Master
Class

ALSO BY PAUL WEST

FICTION

O.K.
The Dry Danube
Life with Swan
Terrestrials
Sporting with Amaryllis
The Tent of Orange Mist
Love's Mansion
The Women of Whitechapel and Jack the Ripper
Lord Byron's Doctor
The Place in Flowers Where Pollen Rests
The Universe, and Other Fictions
Rat Man of Paris
The Very Rich Hours of Count von Stauffenberg
Gala
Colonel Mint
Caliban's Filibuster
Bela Lugosi's White Christmas
I'm Expecting to Live Quite Soon
Alley Jaggers
Tenement of Clay

NONFICTION

The Secret Lives of Words
My Mother's Music
A Stroke of Genius
Sheer Fiction — Volumes I, II, III
Portable People
Out of My Depths: A Swimmer in the Universe
Words for a Deaf Daughter
I, Said the Sparrow
The Wine of Absurdity
The Snow Leopard
The Modern Novel
Byron and the Spoiler's Art
James Ensor

Master Class

Scenes from a
Fiction Workshop

PAUL WEST

HARCOURT, INC.
New York   San Diego   London

www.harcourt.com

Library of Congress Cataloging-in-Publication Data
West, Paul, 1930–
Master class: scenes from a fiction workshop/Paul West.—1st ed.
p.   cm.
ISBN 0-15-100574-5
1. West, Paul, 1930– 2. Fiction—Authorship—Study and teaching.
3. Teacher-student relationships. 4. Authors as teachers.
5. Workshops (Seminars)   I. Title.
PS3573.E8247 Z464 2001
808.3'071'5—dc21   00-049866

Text set in Spectrum
Designed by Lydia D'moch

First edition
K J I H G F E D C B A

Printed in the United States of America

Contents

Contents

Contents

A prose writing seminar with the legendary and ferocious Paul West, this class would, as they say, change the course of my life. Every Thursday afternoon, I left the magazine office and ventured downtown to the conference room where the class was held, as self-conscious of my hose and heels as of my non-degree student status, my stuttering stories. Paul, dressed in soccer shorts and a pink oxford-cloth button-down shirt, held court at the end of the long table and frequently fiddled with the air conditioner protruding from the wall beside him. Arrayed around the table, the motley assortment of graduate students vied for Paul's attention, alternately leaping into the conversation with passionate conviction and leaning back with an affected air of nonchalance. I had no idea what was going on, but Paul's continually fascinating commentary held my attention fast. Though I floundered, I was not bored, and, so, even though I received my share of harsh criticism, I was hooked.

Within a matter of two months, I went from cranking out soured romance stories to crafting a bizarre and tortured experimental piece about the experience of hypoglycemia, and all the credit goes to Paul, who pushed hard, whose spoken vocabulary wheeled like stars in the firmament, who gave me a photocopied page of Proust with the instruction to read it every night before I went to sleep. None of the other students in that first seminar knew what to think when I showed up with this wild piece of writing—it had outdone their critiques based on my status as an unimaginative dullard trying to edge my way into their ranks. At the beginning of class, a fidgety silence fell, and a few ventured mild reprimands for my having broken all the rules they'd said I'd followed too closely before. Paul, however, who has Type 2 diabetes himself, and, even more important, loves any flight of lingual fancy, became at once my friend and champion. "'Flours,'" he noted about one phrase in the piece, "I've never seen that used in the plural before. Bravo." Breakthrough.

—Lisa Roney, *Sweet Invisible Body*

Remembrance
of Things Proust

🐾 Bayeux, So Lofty

A man of imagination among scholars feels like a sodomite at a convention of proctologists. So I keep away as much as possible from buildings named Burrowes South and Goldwin Smith, and their denizens. Presumably the sense of pageantry fails us in these places and memory works its vapid trick, leaving glamour to literature and other arts. A room named Goliath or Aesop might have won me over, but where would you find such a thing?

My off-campus seminar room is seconds away from my bolt-hole, and I can shuffle down to it in bathrobe and slippers if I want, electing my own form of hibernation, or in summer shorts. "He doesn't even dress to teach" goes one vengeful old canard, while another reports my inability to meet a four o'clock class, having overslept. All true. So, I have been waiting, ready for last year's repeats, considering the old gang of MFA students almost as my children, plus just a few newcomers. The talk will be of earlier years and years to come and my brain will fix on something alien, the *pseudomonas radiodurans* that thrives amid the neutron flux and Cerenkov radiation in nuclear reactors, just to keep the ship of self steady during the onrush of memory from a pent-up year I taught.

In the beginning I just sit and wait for them to slink in, Mark often first so as to get his quotes from Thomas Mann ready, diabetic Lisa often last, breathing hard from some earthenware embryo of a class called Verbal Technics, she apologizing and me protesting, "You hardly need us anyway, any more than any of the others need the rest," and down she sits with a becoming flush to her cheeks as if rain-lashed, and I wave, "Sorry about the cookies, a bourgeois habit, you know. Don't unpeel the top, just slice it off with sturdy scissors if you have any handy." We are a Brownian motion of blissfully autonomous spring crocuses coming up afresh weekly.

I am getting my mind together against the wacky drift of pensiveness, at last moved to gripe, "There are too many of you, I am going to lower the boom next week," but I never do, there are too many shining afternoon faces, they have been reading the same page of Proust all night and are going to tell me all about him while I sit in mules, blue shorts with a yellow stripe, a diet something-or-other by my right hand. It all begins before it really begins, it always does, First Lisa gesturing with a comb as she says, "He wakes you up while keeping you asleep." I know she expects some answer even as they devour the chocolate cookies first, like schooled wolves, and continue with bronze mouths.

No one begins, not even Mark, so I launch a bit about Stravinksy, wondering what, in *Apollon Musagète,* the newborn Muses are born *from.* Nobody has heard it, so I should have brought it to play, but I switch to Proust, as I should, having inflicted him on them: "Why do you think he thought it was always better, in all situations, to bring a tureen of mashed potatoes along?" Some bright spark whispers behind a hand.

I move on, asking them what mashed potato has to do with Proust. Anything to get started. Now they begin to rise to the bait, invoking slop, pottage, paste, gruel, cream, a silver tureen, malleable prose, soft flesh, and we are away into the hinterland of the red herring. Now they are willing, some of them, to buy Proust's earthiness, where the potato comes from, and his habit of treating chamber groups that pleased him to lashings of creamed spuds. Michael, born amanuensis, is writing something, no doubt to counter me with a year hence when I have forgotten all, retired to ruin a new typewriter.

I remark their animation, thinking I could slide out and leave them to it, they have transcended me, who come to them along the same hallway, informal to the point of raggedness. First Lisa, tall and groomed with a face that has not been in the weather, offers me a cookie with a long, typist's hand, at the same time canting her head away from me to counter Nomi's "Oh, I thought it was trite," and the babble begins, fueled by sugar and caffeine. Didn't he lead a beribboned pig through the streets of Paris? Asked Calvino if *Italo* was why he wrote in italics, see. Says you have to wait months and months. No, it was Huxley who said it, the doors-of-perception man. Long before there was any Gestapo. It's called showy sedum — it opens out wide, then goes red.

All this has come from afar to be focused here, with me far from in control, and I have learned to cherish the discharge of energy kept quiet for a term, but husbanded and honed for exercise like a prancing toy dog in this very arena. Perhaps the air conditioner is their catalyst as I sit with one hand on the controls, like Moustache who drives a locomotive from Istanbul to Paris, cranking the levers and dabbing the sweat. Outside, winter rain is dawdling to a pearly halt. "Should *I* go first?" "*I'll* go instead, I'm not so nervous today." Michael and Nomi are having a little debate: After you, Claude. No, after you, Cecil. We try to begin.

"Instead of cookies," Christina is saying, "we could have a big tureen of mashed potatoes, slap it out with big spoons onto paper plates, and mayo — you gotta have mayo." In the corner, someone else, First Lisa, says, "You could see the little husks piling up as the spider caught them and sucked them dry. I'd sooner have a bedroom full of birds, sitting and warbling, y'know." Her grave, studious face seems to wrinkle, or is it crinkle perhaps, and she makes the motions of flying birds, at the same time with ample scooping gestures enclosing the shape of a big tureen. The others laugh and ask for a Proustian tureen, no more cookies. "Please, let's live dangerously!" Quelling that little riot, I restore us to the text in hand, which has mysteriously appeared on the table, warm from folded-up habitation near a palpitating part of the body. Why do they carry Proust so near the heart? As if he would give any of them, being the snob he was, aloof and aeronautical and snippily predatory, the time of day. I am here to make a point about place-names and to remind them to read intimately into them, make them live the lives of the people who have lived among them, but am I doing it? As locally, I explain, you could surely make something out of Bellefonte, Altoona, and Clearfield. How like Langland *Clearfield* is! Now we are moving, even if only from A to B, or from B back to A. I am Uncle Paul.

Page 422

Still puffing up that hill with cobblestones in Baltimore, where I go to read from my fiction and then in a huge auditorium to address assembled doctors on my recent illness, where for some reason I ad-lib the whole thing, reading quotes aloud and then expanding them. At the end, a well-known local shrink comes up and says I have a well-wired skull, which I am afraid isn't half as good as telling me I excelled at cricket, but he's seen something, got something going: I freewheel, as I always do. After this, several doctors bring down the ramp some recently operated-on cancer patients, with whom I have humbling talk, making me think of an earlier day when, to get examined for a pensionable Air Force injury, I entered a room full of legless and armless men, the halt and the blind, and never went back. I am almost tempted to tell First and Last Lisas, Joe and Mark and

Michael and Dimitri and Christina, and Nomi Eve about this, but hold back for fear of being ghoulish on Proust's day, the ills of my body none of their business; they have bodies of their own and abysses to cross. So I am not always as thorough as I should be about my theory of humanity, that we are nature's raw material to be shaped into grotesque works of art. How tell them that with their eyes on the bright savannahs of hope, *on* meaning *aimed at.*

I look at them, a vehement motley, trying to group them in my head, but they have conspicuous personalities and will never be interchangeable. "I'd question that," Dimitri, former assistant sheriff of New Haven, is saying, no pistol in hand, to Christina, of course (they're an item), but she just looks through him, her mind on Vercingetorix. First Lisa is chortling, "I know the whole damned page by heart," while Last Lisa shakes her head and seasons her stare as I wonder if these two, named alike, are going to be allies. Joe has a grave, coal miner's glare, knows he is not going to vary or wobble, not even when Mark skims the surface of his knowledge and says, "Big verandahs with rocking chairs, how'd you like that for what ails you?" "Not on your life," says Joe, coughing on aniseed. Nomi hears them and asks, "Where is he?" "Who?" Michael. "Vince, brother of that boxer," she says, ever alert to relationships. They are a hubbub, a maelstrom, a ferment, graced by wit, Dimitri so pale, Christina also pale in the olive Italian mode, the Lisas giving each other not the evil eye but the eye skeptical, perhaps intuiting a rivalry beyond nomenclature, Nomi too hearty for words, Mark, in whose face German and Welshman fuse, yawning merely to remove air. "*Vince,*" they shout, "we can't begin without Vince," who strolls in on cue while I tell them we've already begun, this is the decline and fall of all of us. Only Michael seems to have the class in hand, quietly signing death sentences in blue fiber point. What does he *do* on those pages?

"Page 422," I announce above the empty cookie bags, more isolated by the copy machine than it ever was before. "Notice, my eager ones, how he dotes on the 1:22 train (have you ever done that?), then like someone using calipers with postage stamps or butterflies, picks out the details, lauding *Bayeux* for the 'old gold' of its second syllable, *Vitré,* whose acute accent makes a bar across its ancient glass, losing one metaphor in another, and then *Lamballe,* whose whitenesses range from eggshell yellow to pearly gray. He finds the end syllables of *Coutances* rich and yellowing even as the syntax begins to break down and he starts using Beckett's hideous semicolon—remember?—before he lets it go, a burst, an explosion, with *Questambert* and *Pontorson,* 'ridiculous and naive,' he says, white feathers and yellow beaks strewn along the road to—well, synesthesia. How about *Pont-Aven's* pink-white flash of the wing of a lightly poised coif, tremulously reflected in the green water of the canal? I asked you to read it at least a dozen times, then stretch it like rubber, you lucky people, maybe until it snapped and you said to yourselves *knicker elastic,* he's filling in; the places, the sites, the steeples et cetera were nothing like. He's bridging. Maybe so. But add them all up and they turn into something larger than their whole. Comments?"

"That's *the* Bayeux, of the tapestry?"

"None other."

"Two yellows!"

"Three!"

"Cutey-poo?"

"That's overdoing it. Exquisite more like."

"At least it doesn't suck."

"Don't you all remember? *Suck* was banned ages ago." Me.

"Imagistic, then, as if he's painting and, just a bit, going outside the lines, not that it's coloring-book stuff."

"Were we supposed to copy?"

"Just to admire."

"Well, when we've admired, do we have to see some principle of procedure in it?"

"?"

"Then it's a kind of orchestration, going sideways while ever so little advancing—forward at a slant."

Vince has been shaking his head all through these utterances as if someone referring to Latin America has omitted Brazil. "It's the *imaginary* landscape of a novel," he says, "before he gets to grips. A set piece."

In a while, I think, none of these utterances will fit the mouths and minds of Michael, Mark, Christina, the Lisas, but will have swum into the amorphous sediment of notions exchanged. After all, Proust next says these images were false for yet another reason. We have been duped by being otherwise duped. Nobody peering at these spots is ever going to come up with those images, not even Proust. What links them is the good old 1:22 *into which I had so often clambered in imagination.* We have been warned.

Producing bigger and bigger blowups of the vital page and therefore of less and less text until I have just a couple of words.

a tower of butter

to play with, as in the quasi-architectural concrete poems of yesteryear, I try to imagine these twenty-one-year-olds at forty, sixty. God, what horror! I shrink back into the present, preferring them as babies, tots, and luxuriate in that mental roller coaster for a couple of minutes while they pore over the blowups, wowing and Jesusing as if they have never seen prose before, their hands kind of itching to write, something, anything, even sign checks, their noses too close to the chiaroscuro, one of them even volunteering to make some enlargements as big as the quadruple table we sit at, but the offer goes begging, this is more immediate, oh yes, and I fancy they just begin to see, mis-see, through Proust's eyes that have watched lurid sex acts with rats in brothels and interviewed presentable young bellhops at the Ritz. They don't need to know, do they? We are here for technique, as the actress said to the bishop. They are holding it in, but I can see the rictus in their chops; the caffeine is working its way through them, the cold liquid is winning, their legs are crossing, they don't want to break up so soon, but the unisex toilet on the third floor is making its Indian love call, and off they go, excused, in twos and threes, to stand in line, to suffer further until divine relief. Only a few, Michael and Mark, seem able to hold out: big bladders or total abstinence, or, perhaps, little siphons in their pants, gathering up all surplus water for eventual disposal on the sidewalk. Look at that man, Mommy, he's trailing water.

The idea is to make the arrangement of the prose unrecognizable (principle first uttered by Mr. Gladstone), then restore each to its proper place in the pattern, maybe holding just one or two back:

Bayeux, so lofty

so as to magnify the contrast idea. Only about the fifth week will I tell them the story of a predecessor, a Canadian who used to go out to the washroom and plunge his head in cold water only to return for more with a white towel swathed around his Sikh head. This was the fellow who went on to write the "Rocky" novels while holding a teaching job in Iowa. Did, I wonder, my teachings of Beckett's fiction unhinge the delicate flanges of his literary apparatus? What brought him so near and yet took him so far? The story I save for the seventh week, also from that literature seminar, was the equally true story about how my students used to write fan letters to Beckett and receive by return autographed copies of his French texts. Would they go on reading him forever, old and gray in the chimney corner, surrounded by rats, intoning the first sentence of *Murphy*? *The sun shone, having no alternative, on the nothing new.*

A moment of discretion comes as I wonder if, like some old soothsayer or balladeer seated near a campfire, I should rehearse once again my opening tale about characters and how, on a rare occasion, I actually called the roll, appending to it some names from Beckett—Molloy, Watt, Malone, all no doubt fresh from the Dublin phone book, only to have the wits in the class answer, but stopping them short with "Beckett," for whom nobody answered at all. A perhaps worse incident came about when, in a literature class, lecturing about Alain Robbe-Grillet's sexy Hong Kong novel *La maison de rendez-vous,* I began to talk about characters who were not in the novel at all but foisted upon it by my own vicarious imagination in a gladsome fit. Who, they asked, is this Grand-Flibert? Who is this Ange-Bébé? From then on, I was careful to keep my interfering mind at bay, not letting it loose within the precincts of someone else's thrill. Now they tell my stories for me, thank goodness, using the vocative in lenient mimicry, and I tell them I am going to invent some new ones, but on paper, including (said with a wink at Shahid the Shiite poet, who sometimes shows up—a grace and favor inclusion, as with First Lisa): "Up at the house in Ithaca, I used to float his breakfast to him across the pool, eggs and bacon steaming among the chlorine clouds! We never drowned it." He nods, licking his lips as he never does in his beloved Kashmir.

Robinson Caruso

Now I am really teaching, apropos of our old masters Marcel, Sam, and Vlad the Impaler, telling them to get what's unique right up front in the sentence, especially the first sentence of all, stuffing the noun behind it like an ocher puppy. "Never begin with a dull phrase," I say, "and don't let anybody persuade you otherwise. *Their* names are not on the final result. So skip what the words mean; they're just nonce words. *Raw with menace and sly in an older tradition than he could remember, Milo spilled the vinegar onto his boots* will serve you better than *Milo,* comma, or, worse even, *he, comma.* Gather up all that is strange in his apparition, a fistful of novelty, and make the reader assimilate it before passing on to the noun or pronoun, thus ensuring the attractive, sensuous part of the statement gets you off to a good start that keeps its momentum all through, shutting out the rest of the world. Make the reader concentrate. Take that lump of candy floss and shove it right in the reader's face. I want a dozen sentences for next time that seem to flirt with an ablative absolute but actually specify without much warning the sensuous overture. *Please. Celibate gusto wetting his eyes, he* . . . You know the rest. It looks like a *with* construction, your ablative absolute, and it is, but disguised; the *he* is not appositional because there's an implicit *with*. Thank god for English and Chinese." It is almost like insisting on the twelve-tone scale.

"English," I seem to have been telling them for decades, "is full of invisible words such as *he* and *it* and *and*—and is the American vice, poor substitute for lyrical deployment over a full skein of grammar. Put invisible words where they belong, in the crevices and interstices, until having done that relentlessly you slip one in, in a salient spot and thus astound every reader: Doesn't she realize she's breaking her own rule? Faulkner will give you pages of dithyrambic humming, perhaps ungraphed, then clinch all that poly-racket with one physical ingot; after pages of rant he writes, in a para to itself, the simple, adroit phrase *I heard you.* It's as if," I seem to be reciting again and again, "all that went before is a big balloon of tendentious gas, against which he will pit his one little phrase. The effect is huge, I think, a cymbal tinkle after much Bruckner." Even if they don't believe all this, it does them some good. Their responses vary from "Right!" to "Maybe so" to "Too much work" and "Why bother?" to "Hemingway." Which reminds me to tell them that, at the University of Arizona, the MFA students asked me if they could please talk about Proust, Woolf, Faulkner, Mann, Beckett, and a dozen others, all of whom had been banned as slovenly, mainly by a man who is now buried in the desert, about whom, after never having met him during my six months, I composed a little ditty:

> Dirt, receive an honored guest
> Who condescended to Paul West.
> Whoever would have guessed
> A vacant Abbey could be crabby?

You know how, during these things, a kind of interregnum comes between frivolous preamble and solid learning, when what's wanted is ideas, maybe flashy and colorful, dangerous even and somehow classic? So I embark on a couple of mental tunes they might have heard before without taking them seriously enough. "Take your average pastry cook," I say, "or stockbroker, barkeep, osteopath, these people aren't going to give what you care about the time of day. How many serious, highminded books are they going to read? That's why we have to make as much as we can of art, aesthetics, taste, magnifying the calling beyond praise, even to the point of talking about nothing else. If you don't, you'll end up with a ne____ that will be that. For instance, whether you c____ plications of the idea, even the brain wave, or ____ perfect right to formulate some such idea a____ between ontological and historical trauma. Why, even Robinson Crusoe might have hit on it. Or Robinson Caruso as some call him. Ontological is the sheer insult to being that life provides, come what may; we all have to deal with it. Historical is what history does to you over and above the basis. Aldous Huxley wrote of ape and essence. Sartre, of existence and essence. Santayana, of essence in a subtler way. Myself, having boned up on these guys, I incline to think of existence as what we receive from Mother Nature, which is close enough to the Sartrean thing, but of essence as not so much what we make of ourselves, surging up in the universe to define ourselves (carving a scar on the universe as Malraux terms it), as the peculiarities that history brings your way. Who is not subject to history? The young child being bombed is subject to it before he knows what bombing is. The Japanese soldier, unaware that the war has ended, lives on as a wild man in the jungle, disbelieving messages left for him, persuaded to come out only in the fifties, an old man reborn. This is about intellectual framework. It doesn't have to be correct, but it needs to be there, or you end up with a mess of pottage. Now look at Proust, deploying whole ranges of society and cliques in the presence of his own self-engulfing sensibility. See the counterpoint?"

"Spitting blood back at *The Magic Mountain*," Mark says in one of his least-rehearsed voluntaries. "I don't see how you can write anything without a—leitmotif to test the trivialities against."

Now Christina, our sometime student of ancient history, chimes in with "Maybe they're all the same thing. Lump it all together and serve it up. Test the biggest conceit against the tiniest wisp of a phrase."

"No Sally?" Something has occurred to Last Lisa; someone is missing, a newcomer who, to put it grossly, has not new-come. Somewhat breathless, but not very, she trots in after, she says, waiting in the wrong room on campus and then failing to establish our whereabouts. "Only MI5 and the OSS could find us," I protest. Then, quite contrary to the intellectual drift of the afternoon (though I did tell them *always* to interrupt: "You must"), she explains that she's just run twelve miles around the town; she's a long-distance harrier with, I presume, no sense of direction. But she's here, and now we're complete. I hope so. We're enough, though Adam Schonbrun, a poet transfer from Israel, still has not put in an appearance, no doubt stranded on Cyprus. We return to our moutons, as the French say, and *trauma* becomes the in word for the afternoon, to be revisited later in a more settled mood. I look around me and wonder if, at their age, I myself had looked so eager, so devastatingly committed to abstruse art in a nonliterary society, before from incessant typing my fingertips became so spatulate they overlap a single key and often type double, *tr* for *t,* or *ty.* A million times? I no longer recall if the seminar's title was fiction or nonfiction; in *my* woolly firmament, all was prose, subject to durable rules and remorseless respect.

Last Lisa's Letter

⚞ Brilliance Injured

A week later, we do not so much leave Proust behind as acknowledge the presence of his fleshy massif behind us, all around us, the Lavender Everest for some. An old colleague of mine, a suave southerner who reviewed books for the *Hudson Review* and dismissed everything as trash, used to teach a seminar on *Finnegans Wake,* settling on a single page for the entire fifteen weeks, rightly (and perhaps righteously) announcing one page of Joyce as an inexhaustible miracle of contemplation. I approved, as I lamented his departure. "If any of you," I tell them, "would like to do homage to a sentence of Proust, extolling its finesse and architectonic, almost as if judging a cerebral bodybuilding contest, I will exempt you from all creative offerings this semester." No takers. Marcel scared them a bit. Joyce less. I hand out a reading list of foreign fiction translated and invite them to sample the exotic at their own expense: "No quiz, no term paper, no probing until you reach the point the *I Ching* calls *brilliance injured.*"

Now I am involved in Last Lisa's recasting of a long letter into a short story, in the optical illusion of the present tense, which proffers a *now* while remaining in the quasi-limbo of the already written. All literary tenses are past, whatever their intrinsic allusion, unless you dote on cliff-hanger time, spraying your prose with dots and dashes, gaps and question marks. "He, er, hovers on the fringe of huff, resolving to slap Golpovich's face or run him through with—is it steel or samite . . . He's pausing again, mind racing, the words forming for either, if he chooses to match word with deed." They laugh at the cumbersomeness of it. It's laborious to do, and tiring to sustain. "You are always," I hazard, "trying to dodge the ghost that says what's couched in the past is commandeered, possessed, but you can just as easily do incertitude or mental wobbling, or being lost for all the mots justes, in the imperfect, the past, or the pluperfect. I nonetheless admit to an uncommon degree of excitement in resorting to the present, when things seem on the point of unfurling, and only then, when it's all molten and nobody, least of all the writer, until the very last spasmic instant, knows what is going to happen. But, you know, the most kismet-bound tense is the future perfect: *Hemingway will have climbed Kilimanjaro.*" I try to enlighten them about the arbitrariness of convention, which is something agreed upon, indeed *convened* upon, but you can see it in their eyes that they like the much-slandered present because it seems to offer them more freedom, something open-ended, an aftertaste of the hot inks the Athenian Greeks wrote in. So I tell them the story of that, how *encauston* became *enque,* and then I recoil to Lisa's letter, one of those swingeing, indignant, terminal epistles we address to an ex-beau, whipping up a curd of loathing beyond the poor bastard's demerits: extremes make adieu easier. She has decided that its double status must end. Letter becomes story, and if so, what are the necessary changes? "None," I guess. "You are writing the story of yourself. You are the protagonist in the fiction, but you will probably want to speculate once you've established yourself as the teller rather than the opponent." She breathes a sigh of not so much relief as swarming power. She has set herself free to advance sideways, as I regularly put it: fiction waddles more often than it toboggans forward. "Didn't Sartre in his fiction days say something about the novel as a toboggan that goes over the crest of the hill and vanishes into a domain of new values? Something like that." Someone I am too slow to see mutters something about new values flying up like partridges when the hunter's gun goes off. I don't pursue this, intent on Lisa's change of role, her shift from bleat to tale to story to the story's manger, in which she can have a romp.

"Revenge," Joe is saying, "is a dish best eaten cold. Is that right?"

"What experience—," someone begins, but is swiftly cut off by the other Lisa, his own Lisa, saying, "She can regard herself as her own raw material and assume a distant, clinical stance."

"Whatever happens to you," I respond, twiddling the controls of the air conditioner behind me, "you can regard as raw material, no matter how degraded, unworthy, immoral you feel. It's all grist for the mill, which may make some of you, let's say the most depraved and abandoned of you"—Adam, at last arrived from Israel, gives a *roué* smirk mimicked by Michael (they have been away and performed abominations)—"actually light out for the territory of life at its worst and submit yourself to unspeakable torments just for the sake of a vivid page or ten. You know what I mean." Mark, already composing his book on twentieth-century literary suicides, Hitler included, he informs us, nods, a debonair Faust. My god, I think, he lives with his grandfather on top of a mountain not far from here and comes down only for this class. Not even for stamps.

Last Lisa can now see her accurate and pointed complaint slithering into the world of medieval *compleynte,* which may or may not include the absurd. She wants, she says, to keep the weapon-thrust aspect of the piece (it used to be a letter) rather than assemble all of humanity's woes. "Cold inventive sadism," I say. "Why don't you ask yourself what will be the difference between a sent letter and a conjured diatribe? Surely the latter will engage in more recollection and less abuse? Why, you might leave out the abuse altogether, maybe fixing it into one word stuck in a salient place, as Faulkner would. Try not *deadhead, asshole, turd-cuddler, snot-sucker,* but *oaf.*" Those old words of abuse haven't lost their impact yet, semipolite as they are, sheltered by some etiquette or blaze of chivalry. I am pondering *cretin,* even *cad,* and farther afield even *lobotomy.* There's *rotter,* too, and *schmuck.*

🖋 *Flare Path*

They seem to be getting it, twigging what I say, although they have encountered this impulsive animal before and become accustomed to the way my mind works, when I import an essentially creative process into the classroom and try to freewheel from there, almost surrendering to the same tangential circus my head becomes as I begin again to write. I can't write while in the midst of a teaching term, so I have all the more reason to force something creative upon them. I feel again the need to explain my meandering ways. "Some of you may know that, at certain airfields, the tower will close down at ten o'clock, say, after the last flight has come or gone, commercial, that is, and late arrivals will then have the option, best taken, of keying the mike to bring the airfield's lights to life again: the reds, yellows, and blues. Suddenly that nearly Christmas-tree display leaps up at you out of the darkness, almost begging you to land now that it has become easy, and down you come. Well, when I sit at my Smith-Corona SL 580 (a given model lasts two years only), that is how my mind lights up. It never happens away from the machine. I have to sit there and show willing. I then become heir to too many ideas and pictures, thrilled but sometimes overpowered. That mental airfield shuts down its lights only when I quit the chair. Does that make any kind of sense to you? It's a glimpse into the foundry, the atelier, in which, if you, or I, provide the articulate sentence-forming, the rest of the display or migraine attack will conduct itself without us. I never go past an airfield at night, or peer at the dashboard of an anchored bike, without thinking I should be at the machine, earning my keep, manufacturing wonders." I'm a cockpit man.

Entranced or discomfited, they stare at the latest fugitive from Wells's *Island of Dr. Moreau.*

"Mercy," Mark says. "Where I come from, you see polar bears."

"I confess," Michael says at his most tentatively urbane, "to a little of that myself." Michael does Nabokovian hotels.

"Oh," says Last Lisa, whose story is on the operating table, "I am reminded of low blood sugar. It's a bit like that at times." I know it is, she and I and H. G. Wells all having had the same disease inflicted on us. I get much less than she, however, from the times I need my glucose.

We get on, urging Lisa to reveal herself in the act of writing the story, choosing her fulminations, her snidenesses, by which we mean letting the leftovers, the bits on the cutting-room floor, back in. Myself, I think the letter is just about perfect, but it trembles with unexplored opportunity, like a fiction writer's military Latin. *Ubique,* says the Royal Artillery motto: *I am everywhere.*

Now Sally, she of the iron lungs, speaks up, as concise orally as in her manicured stories. "I think we have to praise her stance in this, standing alone in a rather bleak loneliness she only makes worse by denouncing him to his face. It isn't generic. I mean, he's not just a bad guy doing bad things to a woman; he comes out as quite idiosyncratic, with vices she might once have been charmed by. This makes her indictment of him rather specialized and even more painful. Or so *I* think."

Response to this, perhaps daunted, is monosyllabic, at least at first.

"Of course." Michael. The leaden echo.

"I wish I'd thought of that." Vince. The golden one.

Slowly, as if fencing for position, they open up and explore the piece's psychology while I ponder a bit of *Medea* I've brought to class, from the Chorus:

> *better a sensible life,*
> *gods' loveliest gift:*
> *no quarrelling,*
> *no wrangles to snare the soul.*
> *no thirst for other sheets.*

I was going to quote it, but decide not to; we have tangents enough. A point is emerging: How would the intended recipient feel, confronted with both versions, the original letter and the embellished story? Surely, some think, he would acquire from the latter a larger sense of sympathy; he would recognize the extent to which he had betrayed her, wounded her. If he saw only the letter, the naked affront, he might just feel angry and leave it at that.

"Then," Mark says, "we should send people our stories and not just letters, to make them behave better? Does this make sense?"

"Only if you're the sender." Who was that? I missed the face. I can see the point, but perhaps we have gone too far into psychology, away from technique. About which I abruptly ask, causing a long silence as they try to switch from Mercator to

Conical. Obviously, we need both texts, and Lisa is soliciting advice, that's all. I read the bit of Euripides for its vision of bourgeois bliss and find them smiling their across-the-generations smile. I end up doing some of it for her, as best I can, counseling her to dwell on things more, repeat them sometimes, to pare the accusatory cited dialogue, to allow her mind to spread out more without losing focus, but somehow shifting the onslaught from blunt frontal to something less minimal, in which the obvious bones show through. "Sometimes," I pronounce, "qua fictioneer, one has to permit whatever can get into the mind at the moment, at least within the allotted limits of the characters chosen. If you see. Perhaps this means to be less business-like, less efficient, but by the same token making what's pungent even more so — mordant, say, of nearly paralyzing severity. It means, really, to hoick the text up a few rungs, away from the blasé ruck of those who think fiction is a jigsaw game, using only characters already familiar. I think of Nathalie Sarraute, who presents much of the subconversation — the *sous-conversation*— those dreary, lazy minimalists omit, secure in the knowledge that they are more like one another than they aren't." Last Lisa's writing it down, against my orders. "Hot ink?" I ask.

"Seething," she answers without looking up, and I wonder if I have said anything useful, ever skeptical of that facile switch from my own habits to theirs. How would *I* do it? Why this is hell nor am I out of it. I'd cast the whole thing from *his* point of view, upon receiving the belletristic letter. He would see her in the mirror when he looks at himself, and then, that accomplished, he would tell the new woman with him a skewed version, putting himself in a good light. I tell her.

"Jesus," she says. "Jesus." Eventually she will receive, today if she is lucky, a scrawled or typed account of her work, and from the assembled class something similar, possibly longer. Weeks later she will present the story in toto or just a few pages. Years later, this very story will appear in the pages of *Harper's* magazine, no hostage to fortune, but like a black Beethoven burned to the bone by the African sun: a final work of art.

Of course, they do not always return to work we have discussed; they just move on, and I, if I am lucky, will receive maybe a year later another version. But not anymore: this is our final semester, as I am going back to full-time writing, with many pent-up ideas to handle. Hence the moments of forlornness I feel as I hold forth among these startling full-feathered professionals, most of whom, in other seminars, I have tried to school in mainly European literature, trying to arrive at a prose poetics of the century, of which only a couple of precepts need to stick: say De Quincey's astounding conceit of the *involute* (a compound experience incapable of being disentangled) or the relegated term *expressionism,* when how you feel about something dominates how you depict it. Two revolutions in one fit! Most of these aspirants have swallowed much of that and prove it in their work, sometimes, say, harnessing a De Quinceyan enigma to a subjective response, much as he himself does in his *Confessions.* If I had my time over, I who began as a poet and critic, would write a book about the seminal, salient De Quincey instead of the one I did do about Byron. If you have spent any time at all teaching literature, the effect will show when you settle in the end for the land of heart's desire: the novel, a prose fiction of a certain length, having as some wag said, something wrong with it.

⚓ *Tsunami*

Off go the bladders after what I am now used to: the huge preparatory sigh as of someone at last sitting down after a hectic afternoon's shopping. Why do people sigh when they hunker down? Is it merely dramatic or is there a true burden released by the lungs, even by the brightest MFAs? When they return, I hand them copies of an obituary, filched from a local paper, of an eccentric who served swamp dinners of pond scum soup, ferns, and raccoon, and chose Cornell as his school because once around three in the morning he saw some students chuck a refrigerator off the Suspension Bridge into the gorge. "It was," says the obit, "the kind of ebullient, even inspirational rowdyism for which he always had a profound respect." What will they make of this poor fellow, born in Pottstown, Pennsylvania, dead at forty-six? I smell a character. Will they? They impound the screed and say nothing. Results in several weeks' time. I have bled a little potassium permanganate into the clear water of their souls. Leave it at that.

"What exactly is the aroma of overused toilets?" I am asking again, knowing full well how awkward smells are to pin down. It isn't enough, I argue, to have a deep sense of myth; a crippling sense of smell is even better. Michael, as if rehearsed, says, "Skunky chrysanthemum," and they let him get away with it, foot on the step, as someone else mutters, "Minty locomotive smoke."

"While you were away, unified," I tell them as they drift back, "I was thinking about the sighs we emit when sitting down, and I think it's symbolism, although I can see how two hours seated helps the bladder lie horizontally to some extent, but when you stand the water drops, creating a new and urgent sensation. The extreme form of this is those people who can sleep for eight hours without resorting to the bathroom. Then they wake up full to the brim. Sorry. I sometimes need to consider vulgar things, as when the exquisite proseur José Lezama Lima in *Paradiso* speaks of a character prodded from sleep by 'divine chocolate,' and you don't quite know if it's cocoa awaiting him, a faex, or some other gastric urge: a trope best left intact." I also had time to recall, from my novel about Doc Holliday, the dentist gunman, how we see the gun battle at the O.K. Corral through the eyes of Doc's cousin, a nun, who has pieced her account together from smuggled-in newspapers as well as his long-delayed letters. After reading her letter, he compares her version of the event with his. "You will see, I hope, how different the two versions are. It's true, he really did have a cousin Mattie who became a nun, to whom he wrote often, but their letters have vanished, so I rewrote them with appetitive delight, hers especially, an anchoress contemplating the frontier. I suppose that's why I was thinking about how Lisa could shift her personages around, revealing him on the receiving end, then filtering his own version through hers as if she had sent him an acre of filter paper. Are we back? Dare we go farther? How would certain writers handle this material? Say Robbe-Grillet, Faulkner, Beckett, Ivy Compton-Burnett?"

"How about your favorite, Sarraute, then?" Michael is reeling me in.

"*One* of my favorites," I tell him.

"Yes."

"She would bring to bear on the uttered, the enacted, the said and done, all the stuff that's wasted in life: the abandoned phrases, the unsaid invitations and rebukes, the ruminations and the self-communings, the viscous mental mess we indulge in all the time, the inchoate and the muddled, the block of molten marble that yields up utterance, so prized by unliterary writers."

"It sounds," he says, "as if somebody deciding or not to mail a letter to his sweetheart would take up an entire novel."

He thinks he has me, but he doesn't. "And who's to say," I suggest, "that all that stuff is any less a part of living than groomed speech, deliberate action? One of the popular delusions abroad on the Rialto is that only the spoken and done reflect the doer. You have to go back to somebody like Dorothy Richardson or even Édouard Dujardin to appreciate the hidden, the banked, the suppressed, all of which figure in life, whatever middle-of-the-road suburban reviewers say."

Now someone asks about Richardson and Dujardin, and I answer, "*Pointed Roofs*" and "*We'll to the Woods No More.*" I haven't time for all that, not here, but their instructors in the stream of consciousness should have at least mentioned these people. How sad I find it that aspiring and virtuoso writing graduates get no kind of an education from the scholars and scholiasts who trot out ritual trinities such as Hemingway, Faulkner, and Dos Passos without the least attention to the huge heaving swell of literature out there beyond the breakwater, the tsunami that's always building. Nor do you find many of these academics in the least interested in Hemingway the athlete of pure will, fanatic of the pared sentence, or Faulkner the supremo of incantatory rhythm, or even Dos Passos the movie writer manqué. I have tried to bring literature to these students but within the damned parameters, though construing "Forces in Contemporary Literature" as widely as possible. They go out into a world where almost anybody has heard of nothing: no Blanchot, no Cortázar, no Janet Frame. I have always emphasized "foreign" authors, mainly because nobody else does, and I tell the story year after year (or I told it) about my being in the offices of the *Washington Post*'s *Book World* and being asked if I would look at all these foreign books in translation, if they're any good. That's how I became an exotophile with a big library of such works, mainly novels, at home among the French New Novel, the Latin American Boom (so-called), and the absurd. "You'll never hear about this stuff," I tell them, "in the outside world, or much in the academic. Cultivate your garden while you can."

I presume they will, though under whose tutelage only God knows. I'm trying to get back to Lisa's ad hoc alterations, along which compulsive irrelevances must figure, and I tell how a certain passage about music in a novel I was writing evoked for me the goblins and elephants E. M. Forster dreamed up as counterpoint to Beethoven's Fifth in *Howards End,* except that my composer was Honegger and the work in question, his piano concertino. The image that came to my mind, in the wake of those goblins and elephants, was of tiny hand-sized horses that kept trying to trot up from the wood frame of the keyboard to the lip of the keys, but always skidded back because the reach was too big. Again and again they tried, several of them, clopping upward and toppling back only to try again. Relevance? Point? Well, a literary allusion for the cognoscenti, I suppose, but—much more obsessive—an image coming right out of the music that wouldn't go away. "Now I know," I tell them, "that people have lived long lives without the merest recourse to classical music, novelists and doctors and accountants among them, and they see no point in evoking it. But *I* do, I always did. My mother was a concert pianist and I grew up in a cocoon of piano music. Hence my free-ranging link to Honegger, who certainly had no horses in mind. To me, the horses formed an idiosyncratic key, without which that particular passage, no more than a paragiraffe, would have had no resonance. Perhaps a trademark. Lisa?" Lisa the Last.

Mark's Nursery

🖎 A Vapid Biker

For some reason I begin our session by thinking about death, at which Mark, who lives atop that magic
mountain of his own, though not spitting red, brightens and
nods. "Have you noticed," I say, not so casual, "how, if you tell
people you have had a death in the family, they condole heavily
and, thankful to have got that done, carry on with their lives,
drenched in denial. Few seem bowled over by your loss, actually
made to envision their own tormented end, on bed or blasted
heath. The destroyer of delight passes them by until he does
not. In one Hemingway story, they hang a storm lantern on the
deceased's lower jaw for the winter, at least until the snow stops

flying. In an outhouse. I must confess that I myself feel more than a paroxysm of cold shudders, a leaking of the eye, almost the sensation of throwing up; but, then, I have a long story, 'The Dark,' in which a man of tortured sensibility decides that the dark matter that keeps the universe from flying apart like those plum puddings beloved of the cruder astronomers is actually the combined weight of all the dead souls, each slightly heavier than it's not. What a grave and wonderful thing to contemplate since nobody has taken either a scientific or a holy stand on it. Myself, an electromagnetic chauvinist, I like to fancy this myth is true, and why not?" Mark has brought us a chapter from his novel set in a nursing home, not exactly a *One Flew Over the Cuckoo's Nest,* but not Beckett's Magdalen Mental Mercyseat either (in *Murphy*).

Since we have all read it, we can begin to discuss, but they hang back as those still among the living will do. "The protagonist," I comment, "is clearly superior to his calling, intellectually, I mean, and so there's an agreeable tension or tenseness between his mental set and the malodorous farce he inhabits. That's good, and you sustain the contrast. Is there not something dignified and stark in a person of whatever gifts subdued to the sludge he works in? Macbeth's hand will the multitudinous seas incarnadine! Dyeing the green one red. Is it the green-one made red or the color green thus converted (it takes a lot of red to do it or you end up with an olive purple). How rarely does the baby rattle of Latin words work so well. Does Mark's persona incarnadine the multitudinous slime therein? It's as if, even in such a gangstery play as the Scottish one, the Latinate sound rescues something fussy and petty, almost as when Wordsworth evokes mundane ephemera in

> "... the heavy and the weary weight
> Of all this unintelligible world ...

"Note the five syllables in that Latinate word, the authentic cry from the heart of professional romanticism afflicted by the Many. I wonder if Mark is achieving a comparable effect in his prose, not in the action, but is he evoking all the lost, wasted golden opportunities outside? The degrees, the CDs, the six-course meals, the thirty-inch screens, the hairy pear of the vulva, the tilt of the shvantz? Not only that, my biscuit-biters: will he come away from this bottom-rung experience blighted, unable to take his place in traditional society? Does it change him, convert him into — if I may borrow from Beckett again — a vapid biker propelling his bike with twin poles and, when asked for his papers, producing bits of newspaper? Or will he go live in a trash can? Will he tie himself to a rocking chair with seven scarves and rock himself to death? Will he die exploded in a bar among the sawdust? It would be an Irish bar, I suspect. As you can see, I have a preference for Beckettian bums, hoboes, derelicts. Laurels or Hardys. In fact, I wonder if there is any other way to go with such an ethos and a bright young man who has been sliced open in an auto accident? Like Mark. Why not put the home — a place where you can feel safe — into Thomas Mann's sanatorium and have the young man fasten himself to a rocking chair on the verandah with only six scarves as the ghost of Samuel Beckett tells the 'gentle skimmer' to be careful? If I were doing it, I'd exploit the huge noble balcony of the Otesaga Hotel in Cooperstown and have a special night for the inmates at the Glimmerglass Opera nearby. An idiot night with Joe Green. I remember playing cricket in the Air Force on the grounds of Ballamona Mental Hospital on the Isle of Man, doctors versus Brylcreem boys, and how the seated uniformed captive audience stirred now and then to an ovation unrelated to play, and invaded the field. Any use, Mark?"

This is Mark's book. By unwritten rules, he should remain silent, but we waive the rules all the time, so he sets forth on his reflexive meander, arguing that I have omitted the chance of his protagonist's staying in the home forever.

"Wouldn't that seem claustrophobic?"

"Well, Beckett does. They play chess. Mr. Endon, whose very name means *within,* plays most erratically."

I try again. "Well, Mark, Queneau said how live in an absurd world? You live absurdly." This is developing well as a snakes-and-ladder sport. Where shall we go now?

"How about," Mark says, his face slightly pink, "the opera coming into the Home?"

"Good," I say.

"And some of the voices being kept afterward."

"Voices?" I love it.

"Singers." OK.

"Question," I say. "Which do you prefer, or would if you rewrote any of it: visiting opera or a night *at* it?"

"Night in, please, then I can import all manner of other stuff—the military, golfers, croquet, a little jam factory, or Jell-O, or even a mini-Belsen."

"Not the last," I complain, "you can do all of that by suggestion and free association. Some of the inmates might have that tortured look anyway."

"They did." He has lived it. Now I ask the others, who have not. One complains that Mark's prose is pedestrian, fails to take advantage of lyrical or vivid moments, has a rushed, palsied air, doesn't provide a magic carpet, isn't Nabokovian. Mark parries, then slices the head clean off:

"Vlad impaled. I am an impala, and the next time you want to bitch about somebody's prose, meet me upstairs at the urinal trough. I weigh two hundred pounds and can wrestle the strongest of patients." How wonderful, I think, to be able to terrorize critics; I recall Dylan Thomas on the steps of the Atheneum in London one December day, thirsting for throat-blood. The critic never showed. I believe Mark, tiptoeing along in the shadow of a certain critic's son, who was beaten up outside the seminar room on a prestigious midwestern campus. They worked him over in the workshop. How apt. Now, where is the energetic Mark amid all this?

"Mark," I ask, "don't you enjoy writing for its *own* sake? Doesn't it make you croon? I mean, as if you were playing the piano, don't you chime along, like Scarlatti?" No, he does not, and I have hit on something Calvinistic in the set of his jib. The adequate may sometimes inspire him, I suspect, unless he chortles with the sheer delight of, among so many monosyllables, the *multitudinous seas incarnadine.* Imagine Faulkner slavering over that. Now the talk shifts from style to action, that extrusion, and I rest.

✒ *The Bloody Horse*

No doubt of it, Mark is interesting, having worked also with Diane Ackerman and William Gass at Washington University, whither he floated on graduation. Then he came back to acquire another MFA. I have driven with him in his preposterous Nazi bomber of a car that stirs wartime memories. He has written four novels already and prefers Pennsylvania materials, perhaps lifting stuff from his grandfather, who presides over an antiquarian society. If incarceration and discipline count for anything, he is almost a fully developed novelist already, occupied by American history, military gear, and the dark shadows of musty boardinghouses. Henry James oversees him, which I think excellent; he will pick up the resounding fertility of the long sentence, the dilute sparkle of socially sapped people. But the prose has to come alive in a manner almost brazen; he has to find out what shades of utterance can fill a penumbra. If James cannot teach him that, neither can I. I fear that he may go on producing his own version of Hindemith's *Gebrauchmusik,* music written to order: what the Brits call *bespoke.* Roy Campbell, one of the livelier South Africans, used to say: "Plenty of bit and snaffle, but where's the bloody horse?" I think Mark needs élan vital, the energy that propels characters through rhetoric and neurosis, the nest of sorrow. I will write on his work that he needs to rewrite one manuscript at a time, bringing to it a lightning rod of saved-up zest. He is brave, chiding me for calling Haydn powdery.

We hit the title, *In and Out,* remarking its closeness to the old in-and-out, although clearly Mark has little that is sexual on his mind. The title refers to patients, of course, mostly in, alas, where there is no more in-and-out—what Beckett on the occasion of asylum calls "music." "It's blunt," I say, "and it evokes. Let it stand, at least until somebody makes you call it *The Life and Times of Carmen Trueblood.*" I am a little puzzled by their disinclination either to take his chapter as straight documentary realism or as some kind of hyperbole: lack of experience, I suppose. I begin to hold forth on a theme I have broached elsewhere, noting how people, because they hate someone's illness or infirmity, begin to hate the ill or infirm person, thus perpetrating a worse injustice. Beckett fastens on this with something approaching zeal, having his inmates indulge in "dry clips"—embraces—that sicken them, so they end up not only loathing their disease, but themselves as well, not to mention the Other.

We all find this uncharitable, but I tell them, "We are dealing here with the algebra of pain; they have gone beyond the norms and deal in a self-inflicted aversion they cannot help, yet at the same time cling to time-honored clasps, the hug, the cuddle, just for the sake of it. In this terrible arena, nothing nice happens, but there are always, as with Sam, the degrees of loathing and disgust, though I must confess I recall no lepers or syphilitics in his work. Mark himself has probably seen more, or thinks he has, than Sam. I do think it's important to keep in reserve, as for a situation too sordid to bear, something like Emily Brontë's notion that the very thought of death and all it entails makes her long for it. That kind of paradox informs a vast amount of twentieth-century literature, at its mildest in the so-called black comedy of the sixties, at its gravest in such a movie as *Shoah* and, in a more palatable way, the Australian novel

Schindler's List. Why, on this very campus, when *Shoah* showed over two nights, there were only about a hundred viewers either night, mostly faculty. I guess the film had no 'entertainment value.' That's shocking, of course, making Beckett's point over and over again for him: People want entertainment, to distract them from a condition they cannot bear to consider, yet have to. If you think literature has no business depicting this, you are no doubt right: it has been confirmed that excitement of almost any kind—delight, horror—is bad for us, so presumably we should avoid every kind of unusual experience."

"What you say," says First Lisa, the one in reserve, who quit her literary studies to write fiction, even after composing a trenchant essay on Beckett, "seems to imply that to have or write literature at all entails a degree of compulsion. We have to be made to want it. Otherwise it's all James Bond. I have heard that in Norway a certain radio station broadcasts in Latin only, and I wonder what degree of enforcement's required to bring the listeners in."

"Oh," I suggest, "you'd have to have *all* the stations talking Latin, then you'd get results."

"How about Greek?" Joe tightening the screws.

"Isn't there," she persists in her lucid way, "something in society, even in progress, that makes us desire the best, even if it's painful? Are we doomed to grovel in the lap of entertainment just because we're too squeamish to envision our own end?" Sometimes her Catholicism shows; I prefer her catholic, at least in class. If you study the lives of the saints too much, you end up soaked in schadenfreude.

"What drives us to be here?" Who's this?

"Natural selection," says Christina, long silent, self-rescued from her Toynbee-afflicted view of history.

They begin to argue in one-liners, then slowly spread themselves out, slinging catchwords — Zeitgeist, teleology, Teilhard de Chardin, Gaston Bachelard, fire and gravity and Valéry's *implexe*—across the table in an almost exact parody of last year's arguments. "We have gone beyond Mark's asylum into the evolutionary guess at progress, hypothesizing a bent for excellence that echoes Goethe's the Eternal Feminine. What is the propulsive force? Why does it affect so few? Is an elite its only product?"

"An elite of pessimists," says First Lisa.

"An elite of disillusioned realists," says Dimitri, perhaps thinking of his own writing.

"The best and the brightest," someone adds, only to be countered by someone redundantly saying, "The most corrupt of all."

"The corruption of the best," Nomi tells us, coming to sudden, translated life, "is the worst."

"OK," I answer. "Where does the best show up in Mark's glue factory? Are these inestimable rejects in a warehouse, or is the best in repose and action inside such folk as his protagonist deliberately sacrificing himself in the interests of the doomed? Is this all about altruism?"

"I think my novel is," he retorts, "if you only read all of it. Taken in the round. Can you conceive of a young man who gets deflected by a noble cause? Who learns in the school of hard knocks, so-called?"

We can, I think, and some of us, I certainly, will be reading it complete. So, *let* his prose be unstylish; he has a philosophical point to make—unlike one woman in the publishing profession, who ought to know better, being a former attorney, who uses "philosophical" to mean "financial," but is too squeamish to use so aggressive a word. Thus, you can have a "philosophical" discussion of sales figures conducted entirely in numbers. I tell them. They recoil and snigger. Is this the divine Rialto toward which they aim? Is this what awaits them if there is life after graduation? I am tempted to tell them that the really hard work begins only after you finish writing, but I don't; they would never believe me anyway, convinced as most of them are that the golden caravanserai of print awaits them around the corner complete with keen editorial minds and benign contracts. What always bothers me is that, when you hone the average into being superior, you are making them less publishable; so what on earth do you do with as bright and gifted a bunch as this, already superior from reading and practice, ready to be, if lucky, virtuosos, some even with a distinctive style, that bright unique emanation from the personality? I have seen the enemy, and they are not ours. Thank Zeus, I say, for the handful of able editors, to whom the MBA remains a closed book, who still think publishing a noble vocation and revel in interior words. I suppress all this, if I can, believing as I must in the quality of prose as some doctors believe in quality of life. And I reserve the right, now and then, to tell some blockhead where to get off, I the "legendary and ferocious" oracle who once told a writing student, now an editor at some magazine, "I would rather lie naked in a plowed field, under an incontinent horse, than read this piece again." Of such disdain is reputation made. Those who enter this room have guts.

"Lexical concision," I say to Mark. "Ordinary words in unique combinations. Song, rhythm, joy." I wonder if, with Henry James looking on, he will heed me and so lift his ruminations on human excess and inadequacy to a level somewhere between *Piers Plowman* and *Brave New World.*

"Bravo, Mark," someone says.

"Bravo, indeed," I tell him. "Never quit."

"I'll write all over it." Joe.

"I already have," says First Lisa.

The table becomes a zone of paper shuffling all aimed at Mark, who gathers up the scrawled-on copies with poignant indifference and stacks them. From now on he will be twice as voluble, not so much getting his own back (what own?) as testing their work against his full belly of world literature. Only the Japanese elude him.

After we adjourn, I hold an informal office hour, a rite they now regard as an extra hour, part bull session, part prophecy. They all sit there as before while I talk to them one on one; it is a tutorial en masse.

✍ Bull

And I do it with inordinate sympathy, knowing some of them have to break themselves of one habit, which to most would-be novelists wouldn't matter at all since to the masses novel writing is typing, never the pursuit of perfection, not even of the Graf Spee. The habit, I believe, is to settle for the first version set down, not pausing (or going back in a month) to make a particular sentence more beautiful. I'll put this in my no doubt obsolete, quasi-Victorian, aesthete's way, knowing I am not only a Luddite (kept from writing with a pen because nobody, not even I, can read my scrawl). I realize that I am in the presence these days of TV commercials that make no sense to me at all. In one, a group of dunderheads are *trying* to come up with words that rhyme with *elation*. Imagine racking your brains for *that*. Is there a weaker rhyme in English? What do they intend? Actually, I am delighted to find this obnoxious aspect of American home life rendered, at least as I see it, more recondite and oblique than Mallarmé. Perhaps commercials will discover symbolist poetry. What a thrill to realize that the nation's commerce now depends on people's ability to decipher some cryptogram of letters and decimal points amid a procession of frames utterly unconnected with one another or anything else: cars underwater being ogled by a bashful goldfish. In a sense, commercials have discovered what *we* call art, at last realizing that customers can be conned with enigmas as much as with brazen jingles. My fond hope is that the entire setup will collapse because nobody knows any longer what the big intrusive beast they have let into their homes wants them to buy; but I suppose that is hoping for too much in a country that is money-mad, as if mere quantity had replaced quality of life. I am musing on this and other elitist matters when I see First Lisa gazing at me with the almost apologetic besieging look that says she wants to make another point, she who strikes me as one of the few serious novelists in her generation. She starts in on the idea of a snotty elite, as I thought she might (sometimes her prose, on the page or aloud, takes no prisoners, and you have to read or listen carefully). When was it, I wonder, that she decided she would swap criticism for creativity because something inside her wasn't getting out, and something important to boot. Her literary essays, brilliant and, to me, French in tone, always had an itchy, plastic quality; no matter how many good points she made in the manner of criticism, she engaged in high, metaphorical jinks of her own, aiming to startle and confound, creating an atmosphere where someone scholiastic would have created a syllogism. So she switched.

I am telling them about the French Catholic novelist Georges Bernanos, whom I studied for a semester at Columbia in a class full of French and Swiss. All of him I read, some in French, including *Dialogues of the Carmelites,* turned into a Poulenc opera, which, in its American version, fills the ending with the thuds of the guillotine. "Bernanos," I say, "used to write at the kitchen table, by hand, between fork and knife, anxious not to disturb the place setting for the eventual meal. He was a self-effacing fellow, see, who often gave his manuscripts away to any enterprising caller. I was always taken by his humility and his sulfuric vision of evil all the way from puberty to senility."

About half a dozen of them remain, the rest having gone on to another class, a bar, a brothel, a baseball game, perhaps even in disgust. I never know. "One of my first editors," I tell them, "at Harper and Row, was squeamish, and once he called me in Wisconsin to say that a certain line had made him retch and would I please take it out." Eyes crinkle, mouths twitch; ours is the era of the dump innocently taken. "He used to tell tales about me, always claiming I had a screw loose. He was wrong, though; I just had a screw tightened up more than usual, more than he was used to in his genteel bourgeois kennel." In class, they talk; in this hour they rashly wish they were me, or someone else.

How easily I warm to this theme, almost as interesting as literature itself. There was one editor who attended a conference in Baltimore and persuaded the *Sun* to interview her, billed as the most significant person there. She was never good at answering mail, and I wondered about this until a friend, publishing with the same house, caught sight of her in her office one day, playing Patience against her computer, which she did on a regular basis. One once-esteemed editor of a literary journal showed up one day with what seemed a score of shaving cuts, and I wondered about his blade until a savvier friend identified the little nicks as "gin blossoms," a phrase I remain grateful for. I hope they take these reminiscences in good part as the essential froth that forms on the intact flesh of a live calling, as the wastage or detritus any serious aspirant is doomed to before finding an able, lucid, high-minded accomplice, an angel of words. I tell them to go read Janet Frame's *Scented Gardens for the Blind* and to avoid the fraudulent scenes with Alan Sillitoe in the middle of *An Angel at My Table,* the movie made about her. "Go see her letters in the Rare Book Room," I say. "We have some."

First Lisa's
First Book

✎ Dyes

Staring at them without ever staring them down (gift's a stuff will not endure), I wonder why some speak up and others don't. Some are performers, others watchers. Some, indeed, are scrutineers, anxious to sniff out the game and appraise the opposition before putting a syllable wrong. Odd how the silent ones express themselves with tacit animation: huge smiles, generous nods, shaking heads, raised finger in admonitory warning of something unspeakable, a cough that plays sentry to some soon-to-be-divulged treasure. They all have to present work, but there is no obligation to speak except, in the rough-and-tumble of the hour, something forced out like a sneeze or a burp. I have learned not to call on those who sit munching, asleep, or frozen. So: we have not heard much from Shahid the Shiite poet, but it will be a New Delhi jabber when it comes, or much from Vince, Adam, Sally, and others. The main current of talk falls into a few hands, mouths, and I am content to let that little temporary aristocracy rule until the tumbrils appear and the guillotine blade creaks upward. I have seen notes passed up the table to me (*Sorry, fearsome headache*) and grades given with speechless candor (C–). I am here to test them while indulging them, no doubt fueling them with quite unnecessary sugar from those cookies, but trying above all *to engage them in literary conversation* above the gut-level of *sucks*. I end up doing much of the talking, which, after all, is what I'm here to do.

In the years since I taught, my MFAs' images have remained bright; indeed, some of them, for being absent, have become more graphic and eternal. The old saw, to the effect that in teaching the students remain the same age while you don't, doesn't apply. The fresco is frozen in time, with only the brains advancing. They keep in touch, and I am proud of them, prouder with each year. With this change: even those who hung back a bit have come forward with age, perhaps more vociferous, more confident, so I am glorifying a gaggle of talents into a fairy circle of geniuses. Their tics and demeanors remain, however, a bonus to time; and the shelf of their books fills up. I recall reading First Lisa's astounding novel, a chapter of which we consider, and thinking how French it is, then mentioning it to Gallimard in Paris. They decline it, but I still join First Lisa with Minou Drouet, who long ago, at the age of twelve or so, shocked the world of France with a novel in which a young girl fed her baby to the farm's pigs. First Lisa does none of that, but her touch of noir is compatible with Drouet's Catholic mania. And if not Drouet, then surely Faulkner or Flannery O'Connor. First Lisa comes to us, after much travail, fully formed.

"Listen to the plot," I begin, "and see what it calls to mind. Fourteen-year-old Camille's mother has died, and she goes to live with relatives, already a victim of sexual abuse. Her presence on a farm for police dogs upsets everyone, and her adoptive parents, the Scofields, treat her just as badly as before. Scofield himself lusts after her while Camille tries to summon up the ghost of her dead mother." The class is goggling. "It's a pornographic ghost story, full of animals, gods, bodies, and injured spirituality." Lisa is already twitching at so bald a recital, but she knows what the reading public is like, even the MFA public, and she has come to class fortified with first novelists' armor: hubris mingled with deep self-satisfaction born of erudite modesty. Then I read the opening sentence aloud, one eye on the group, the other on Queen Victoria:

"Caught in that hour of paralysis called sleep, when the mind wakes to recognize it, panics, and struggles to regain control, when the mind says *Move,* and believes it has been obeyed, only to find itself trapped in its immovable body, when the mind realizes that it's exposed, now not just to this world, but to the next and all the unknowns in between, I prayed that my mother would fold me up in my mattress.

"The chapter's title," I tell them, "is 'The Smell of Indian Dyes,' and the narrative comes from four different voices." Catching myself off guard, I go right on, explaining what I get from this Cartesian roundabout, with its loopings and circlings over and through the pineal gland. "Here is the underbelly of discourse that Sarraute introduces, at the same time as the almost phila-telical attention to the world of things, as if, properly attended to, it will yield up some magical secret. This is the *chosiste* ele-ment, the obsession with *things* that counterpoints the inchoate flow beneath. What I find interesting in Lisa's work, and some of this is cogent stuff indeed, is that she does both without becom-ing a phrasemaker. She spells things out, she doesn't distill, and this I find very French. Your stylists are not French; they're the Durrells and Becketts and Wildes and Frames, the Sir Thomas Brownes and Robert Burtons, and so on. This gives her work something indefatigable, almost a detective touch, the gum-shoe carefully tracking the truth. Your stylist or phrasemaker has a touch of impatience, wants to do it in four words or three rather than two dozen, and expects readers to prize the brevity and intensity of the telling. I think you're born a stylist or not, with not much hope of changing horses, so I predict—danger-ous game—that Lisa, for all her merits, isn't going to erupt into the impatient lapidary. It doesn't matter, but you do need to know what your binoculars are going to bring you, in this in-stance almost a *Rashomon* of spurious factuality.

"Now, at one point," I go on, "not in the pages before you, she actually displays a flicker of what she isn't by amassing the words *gustatory, logotype, malapropism, mansuetude, mnemonic,* and so forth, evincing some kind of haste, or passion to compress, but her usual mode is to spell things out, not strike to the heart of things with a few-syllable phrase. Sorry if I seem to be laboring this, but, when the García Márquezes start calling the French New Novelists cowards for their doting emphasis on the inanimate, on surfaces, you have to have your bearings. This is a brave endeavor, as you can tell from chapter 1, but there remains this to be said: It's almost a novella, which attests, does it not, to some degree of cold compress. She does it all in, as I know, some two hundred typescript pages, and beguilingly so. You know what they say in this country about the novella, a form I myself have tinkered with? It's an un-American activity, whereas the so-called blockbuster—well, you know all that, even if the ultimate outcome is a monster flab of ectoplasm concocted by Max Bupkiss, whose reputed novel is a surgical boot full of Frank Norris.

"Not finished yet," I tell them. "Not quite." I am thinking of Hemingway's bumptious, only half-mock-serious 1949 letter to Charles Scribner about Tolstoy and others. "He wouldn't fight 'Dr. Tolstoi' in a twenty-round bout," I tell them, "because he knew Tolstoy would knock his ears off. But, he said, he would take him on for six, *and would knock the shit out of him and maybe knock him out. He is easy to hit. But boy how* he *can hit. If I can live to 60 I can beat him. (MAYBE)*

"As my old, late friend, the literary critic Philip Young, of this very university—" I begin thus, but halt to envision Phil in his office stopping and then resuming typing throughout a plague of interruptions: our Hemingway man. I resume: "As Phil suggested in the revised edition of his Hemingway book, E. H. was never the competitor but the antithesis of Tolstoy. 'Style in Tolstoi'—even in Russian, we are told—'is fairly inconsequential. . . . But in Hemingway style is foremost.' This seems on the ball to me, and he is right: Hemingway's proposed twenty rounds are a redundant ballet, like the six airily proffered. The truth is that Hem was the superstylist—not the only one, thank god, but one who cared almost savagely about the beauty of his prosaics. Which is what we are here to meet about."

"Not machismo, then?"

"Only as superhuman effort in scrupulous art."

"More like a Zen koan, then?"

"Maybe."

"Closer to Proust, say, than we'd ever supposed."

"Of course."

"Almost dandyish?"

"In a swerving, sculptural, delicate way, yes."

"Well, he never gets much credit for it."

"Not until Mr. Young," I say, "who in one of his footnotes excerpts a page-and-a-half sentence about the Gulf Stream from *Green Hills of Africa,* calling it 'one of the finest sentences Hemingway ever wrote.' Or Proust. Nelson Algren remarked of it, 'Call that babytalk.' Hemingway on the Gulf is close to Joyce on the Liffey except that Hemingway uses lyrical swing rather than algebra. At his best, as Young says, he turns base lingo into gold, ever the scrupulous refiner to whom James Joyce once said, 'I often think that what I write is so damned suburban.' 'A spot of that lion-hunting,' observed Mrs. Joyce, 'would be the thing for Jim.' Do you wonder that the Finca Vigía in Cuba was awash in books totaling some nine thousand by 1960? You get my drift?"

✎ Symbols

There is a spatter of uncompleted questions, as if birds are taking off and then, as a squadron, abandon the attempt and flutter to earth again. I seize the delay to add something they are not going to: "Let me say something else, then I'll desist. She exploits the mystagogical side of religion here, more perhaps than some of us would like, which means she uses religion to limn a private relationship with the universe, a bit like Wordsworth's or Blake's, say, and you may not be able to follow her into it. You may wish to, but you may feel deterred by symbols that don't explain themselves. Remember, in Greek *symballein* was the throwing together of stuff, the hint and the drift; a symbol to us is an adumbration of the unsayable, which Beckett with typical humor calls the *ineffable*. You can't *eff* it, see. You may eff it, perhaps, but your effing won't mean much to others. What a lovely idea the ancient Greeks had, of combining, fusing, clue and answer. For them, the world came together and stayed thus; it wasn't fractured. Well, Lisa's world *is* fractured, and quite often, as with all believers, we are left with symbols only, that may entice and cheer, hearten and brighten, but won't take you to the heart of the unsayable. Symbolic writing is a ritual, at its best in Rilke. What *are* those damned angels of his anyway? At its worst in the novels of Thomas Hardy, with such banter as *the President of the Immortals had finished his sport with Tess.*"

People have circled a mantrap with less circumspection than Lisa's readers approach her chapter. She seems a private person with a private book, and the more she spells things out, many of them mundane and everyday, the more they think she's getting at something obscure. "Actually, this kind of *nouveau roman,* as the French call it, thrives by virtue of the polar light that enters into it, illuminating all things with a harsh, irrefutable finality. You get what you see, even though there seems something huge behind it. Robbe-Grillet sets one narrator in front of venetian blinds, which obstruct his vision all through, and he doesn't budge; in another novel, he sets a soldier tramping through the increasingly confusing streets of a city unknown to him. He is on leave. It doesn't take much to impose something ordinary on the willing reader, enlarging and amplifying until a mere sense-datum has become a metaphysical affliction: the blind, the snow, both writ large."

Now, suddenly, I think I see why some of them never speak until they have had their day in court: bad or good, it will have blooded them, even the old-timers to whom each semester is newborn, with no hung-over confidence from last time. Lisa will speak up, of course, but she's supposed to listen to *them,* without (I insist) necessarily answering. If a piece of work proves enigmatic, the author has the right to leave it at that. Puzzle it out if you can, as Édouard Dujardin does, tracking a mind or psyche for six hours just for the sake of doing it. No denouement, no peripety. All those old and unfictional Aristotelian concepts have been left behind, even by someone such as Thomas Carlyle, whose *Sartor Resartus* in many ways foreshadows Joyce.

"OK, you horsemen and horsewomen of the apocalypse, what do you think?"

"Brilliant." Vince, heaving into action at last.

"Bowled over." Sally, whose prose is as lapidary as you would ever need.

"It makes you want to read on." Adam, the poet with the cordial, bearlike manner. "Not that it would lead you anywhere."

"Maybe so," I answer, realizing that I have no means of plumbing "Christ's body" when she says it, and I have old Bernanos under my belt, not to mention Mauriac's *Thérèse Desqueyroux.*

"Amazing, then," I add, "that she compiles so much every-day stuff, the sort of thing anybody in the street would say, except there's a thunderbolt with it. I mean this kind of thing." Balancing the sheaf of pages in one hand, I tilt for the overhead pearly light that buzzes. "*I look like you, Mom . . . You're too big for this, she laughed . . . You, you'll live to be ninety, like your father's family . . . Four years will pass in no time, Marge thought.* It's weird, as if you were ascending a belfry tower and the higher you went, the more balsa wood there was in the rungs of the ladder. Something like that. She sets you walking high up as if you don't weigh anything at all. My own theory of this, lord help me, is that, because she manages to infuse so much religious feeling into their minds, she can haunt you with ephemera, which always seem to mean more than they say. You might even add to that the fact that those old Greeks said *ephemeroi* when they meant people—we every bit as transient as clouds, sniffles, rheumatism, or bark, steam, the fragrance (nutty-glycerine) of a freshly sharpened pencil. *Ephemeroi* were ephemeral, too. Imagine the dizziness of a Great Victorian, a straw clutching at straws; ephemeral-feeling folk clutching at ephemera!

"For having built dream into the four narrations that form the book, she creates a carte blanche that lets her get away with a neutral, undemonstrative tell, almost as if she were doing one of those callow kitchen-sink English novels of the sixties. She's not, of course. The question remains, however. How much can an unbeliever get from *Body Sharers* without pretending to be Christian? I mean, can you contentedly live among the prosaic symbols without assimilating what they mean to her? I'm not sure I know, but I must confess her odd mixture of plain prose with visionary intensity gives me a workout on the level of prose aesthetics."

Shahid, one of our two gate-crashing poets—whose dissertation under my none-too-gentle hand has been about T. S. Eliot, whose name almost spells *toilet* sideways—launches into a response worthy of her controlled zeal, importing into the discussion the objective correlative and some dark matter that profoundly upsets Hamlet. He gives an Eliotian response, which is all right by me, eager as I am to find my way in. He thinks Lisa has done well to "dumb down" her language so as to throw her theology into stark relief. "If she had written it up purple," he says, "you would have had Wagner on top of Mickey Spillane, or Bruckner on top of Sade. In other words, her intuition of counterpoint serves her well. If you are eyeless at Gaza, you can always hum to yourself."

They fall on him like wild dogs of the African veldt, glad to have a proxy target, but he swerves away, circles back, and bites them in the haunches, suavely sly with his heart still in troubled Kashmir, his poetry reaching along a long landline to New Delhi. He is enough of an expatriate to have a focus on

Lisa's prose, which presents a Christ at least as remote as Rilke's angels. With a passion for, as he calls it, "showing off," he responds well to riposte and usually wins out from being better read; but he doesn't always show up (being a doctoral candidate), and when what we need is an urbane sardonicist he isn't there, and the gap gapes. Shahid, the missing formalist.

Now Mark, every bit his equal but not as serene a performer, asks him about Hamlet and what Eliot thought his trouble was—other than his father's brother having married his mother. Shahid does his equivalent of a mental curtsy and quite rightly explains that Hamlet, unable to spell out the brute facts, has to trump up something else he *can* manage. Sex perhaps. Or his own hesitant personality, thinking too precisely on everything. Mark invokes Hitler's failure as a painter, and they are off, into a circular Q-and-A worthy of Lisa's first paragraph.

Aside

Now Dave, whose face has undergone various pauses—eagerness, urgency, impatience, frustration—on the way to an outburst, at last breaks his mutinous silence and cranks our ship of stateliness firmly to one side. "May I take us somewhere else?" The author of numerous published stories, he is writing a dissertation on experimental fiction and recent science. I am surprised to see him in the role of inquirer. "If you promise," I tell him, "to let me down lightly if you ask about the second law of thermodynamics. Things run down?" "Oh, that," he says. "I was wondering if I might put a couple of questions to you about fiction."

He asks about the French New Novel, wondering where it fits in the general field of fiction, and I begin, excusing myself for repeating what some of them have heard before.

"Actually," I say, "it did better here than in France, to begin with, maybe because, in France as in England, if a thing's been done before, then it's welcome to be done again, whereas if it hasn't, it's taboo. Or perhaps it's because in this country, oddly enough where the novella is unfashionable, even distrusted, some foreign fashions catch on. I'd very much like to know the answer to that. One twenty-page term paper explaining it will get you off all hooks. Anyway, the *chosiste* novel, the novel of thingness, harks back to the nineteenth century, first to Balzac, who thrived on meticulous delineation of interiors, then to— something I construe as Victorian—the passion to have something fixed to hold on to when all the rest is in motion. Those old whiners, Ruskin and Pater, desired it most of all, so you might say there was and still is something fortifying about peering at an utterly still object—a font, say, or a lintel, a ladder, a candle, an empty cage—that has no opinion of you. If you need the French version à la Sartre, you can separate the world into what he called the *pour soi* and the *en soi,* meaning consciousness and thingness, self-awareness and lack of it. Sartre shows a young man staring at a park bench that refuses to stare back at him, and Abram Tertz (pen name for the Soviet dissident André Sinyavsky, pallbearer at Pasternak's funeral) reveals a young idealist in the act of hating his bedside table because it will outlive him." They are writing again, which I find daunting because I am speaking impromptu, but a swig of diet Coke lifts me up again to even more reckless plateaus.

"Yes, Michael?"

"Would you please repeat that Russian name?" I do, happy with a memory of having taught *The Trial Begins* in my comparative literature seminar, Tertz epitomizing the antitotalitarian, Sartre, the anti-ontological—against being in toto, or even more accurately, existence.

"Again, if you'll bear with me, what you find in such writers, and there are at least a dozen more, from Butor to Pinget, is the homesickness of no longer possessing that unity of the old Greeks, when the two parts of symbol came together fused for all time. Or so they hoped. Thrown together: the image and its meaning, which makes you wonder how precise their yearnings were, how pinned down were their notions of spirituality, courage, zeal, say, and especially, if you go back to Plato's divided line that looks like a TV antenna, with on one side the receptive faculty and on the other the thing perceived. Thus, on one side of the divided line, you find *icon,* on the other *eikasia,* the specialized state of mind receptive to icons."

	THE GOOD		
		D	Intelligence (*noesis*) or Knowledge (*episteme*)
INTELLIGIBLE WORLD	Forms		
	Mathematical Objects	C	Thinking (*dianoia*)
WORLD OF APPEARANCES	Visible Things	B	Belief (*pistis*)
	Images	A	Imagining (*eikasia*)

"When I was an undergraduate, reading *The Republic,* I used to wonder if the cheerfulness of the Greeks about their notion of symbol signified only that they had a rather hazy idea of certain concepts, and the symbol didn't really fuse, mesh, subsume the sign and its possibly ineffable meaning as much as everyone hoped. Maybe, shall we say, they were rather accepting because they wanted it to be so. They, no more than we, found it hard to eff the ineffable, but they, you see, needed to console themselves more. A certain mushiness appears in Greek myths, a mushiness that incidentally comes full force from Gilbert Murray's fruity translations of the tragedians. I recall how savagely Eliot blasted Murray for making Swinburnian slop of Euripides."

Does Dave want me to go on, riding an old hobbyhorse? Oh, yes, they see, glad to leave First Lisa's novel where it was, stranded between *Moll Flanders* and Minou Drouet.

"So," I resume, "you might call the French New Novel a discovery, a bit arid and clinical, but also accurate and responsible, the work of minds trained in the sciences, as Robbe-Grillet himself was. These novelists are far from phrasemakers, being explainers and observers only, always willing to spell things out and therefore akin in some ways to the minimalists, who, so far as I know, have no literary insides other than laziness and an addiction to thin prose. The complementary opposite, of course, would be Sarraute, the French Virginia Woolf whom Woolf actually snubbed—rivals, you see. Sarraute, whom you really ought to look at, fills in the mental hinterland, eschewing the strict little annotations of the *chosistes,* the stern and humorless lab reports of the Robbe-Grillets. Clearly, what she boils up within belongs in the mostly ineffable side of symbolism, and she manages to eff it without making it necessarily meaningful.

I hope all this means something to you; people talking about Walter Scott and William Golding will never get near it because it isn't cricket, if you see my drift. I happen to adore cricket as the most dangerous game in the universe, but I deplore the middlebrow habits of British novelists, and their refusal to let the novel evolve, in almost the same way that cardiology has. Any good, Dave?"

I can see how Q-and-A, if that, may satisfy the old academic yearning to understand, fostered not so much in the ateliers of the MFA as in the university at large. The hunt for meaning never ceases, whereas, see De Quincey, the taste for involute or enigma is an acquired one. Indeed, I tell them, "De Quincey's involute is perhaps a symbol that doesn't work. Now, if you have a symbol that doesn't—Lisa's novel abounds in them—*whose* letters in all your literary education might help you to come to terms with that fact? No prize for guessing."

Shahid, the well-bred renegade: "Rilke?"

"Excellent, but someone writing in English."

A congested murmur begins as they turn to gaze at one another, seeking the answer, whispering (I hear "Blake?" and "Beckett"); they're on the right lines.

"*Keats*, then." Nomi Eve knows her romantics.

"Behold," I say. "Let's see if I can quote the thing. When a man, in the midst of mysteries, doubts and confusions—"

"Negative capability," says Adam, surfacing.

"He's lauding Shakespeare," I say, beginning again: "'When man (sorry, ladies) is capable of being in uncertainties, Mysteries, doubts, without any irritable reaching after fact & reason.'

There! I must say, I like 'irritable.' You see, you have to put up with the involute; your training won't help you. That's what Camus meant by the absurd: the gap between the mind that yearns and the world that disappoints. Keats calls this the Vale of Soul-making. That's what he praises in Shakespeare, whom he calls the only lonely and perfectly happy creature God ever formed. There's a weird story that perhaps makes the point in another way, enabling you to adjust to the vagaries, the dead halts of fate. There was a man who loved puns and always sent in his best ones to newspaper contests, but he never won. So, disgruntled, he put ten together and sent them in to the same contest, certain he would win this time. But he didn't. *No pun in ten did.*"

When the groans subside, I know that the pun, effective in a score of ways, actually stops time, dislocates the educational system, uproots helpful language, and induces a loutish chill among human listeners.

"And," I add, "if the Vale of Soul-making sounds too ethereal for you, remember that Keats's bawdy included such words as *cordial* (semen), *Bower* (vagina), *yard* (penis), *kit* (male parts), *stone* (testes), *stifled* (penetrated), and *Valle Lucis* (pudendum). He seems to have covered the waterfront.

"So," I say to First Lisa, whose Gallic novel has set all this going, "are you now committed to be Sri Lankan or Bulgarian?"

"Ceylon," someone whispers, "Singhalese. Serendip."

"Horace Walpole," someone else whispers.

Who are these whisperers? Am I the involute, unmaker of their mother-of-pearl souls? A couple of French students, patently bright, told me a few years ago that nobody in France heeded Ravel, Debussy, and Fauré anymore, and I disputed that, having arrived in Paris one afternoon, taken to a hot tub, and heard on the radio a sultry woman announcing several hours of "*la musique de l'extase.*" All three of them.

A Prosaics
for Prose

✣ The Page

"Strange things happen to you in France, especially if you go on television (which can be a pleasant experience if it's the show called *Bouillon de Culture*). On something called *Caractères,* I encountered a French novelist touting a book he'd written in both Latin and French, *Albucius* the title. Rather ponderously he explained to his huge electronic audience the language switch, and I suggested he do it in twin volumes, gradually increasing the Latin in one and the French in the other in a variety of ways, from chapter alternation to macaronic sentences that jumbled both languages together. This peeved him so much that he slung his earpiece at me, which, being tethered, bounced back at him. It was obvious that he did not relish humor about his work and expected to be treated with enduring reverence. Myself, I thought it was a good idea, though not one *I'd* practice."

The class did not smile at this tale, and not even Nomi, who knows Latin, found it beguiling. I wrote it off to privacy, something worth treasuring but unspoken ever after. They much prefer something like the true story of the American novelist who, going from Buffalo to New York by train with a neatly wrapped sandwich in his kit, feels too embarrassed to unpeel and eat it and arrives hours later with a grumbling tummy. Ah, the gaffes we think we have denied ourselves! It is time to relinquish France and its ententes, cordial or otherwise, for something nearer home.

They let you get away with nothing, however.

"I don't see how you'd do it," Shahid says, and I see Sally nodding, taking an unlikely lead from New Delhi.

"You need a halfway point," I tell them, "after which you increase the amount of the other language."

"Wouldn't work, Paul." Perhaps Shahid is thinking of rearranging his dissertation in just this manner. I see his point. To manage the crescendo of the one language and the decrescendo of the other is almost impossible, certainly if you want the result to be seamless.

"I suggest alternating, so that the reader would read one page in French, say, then one in Latin, but that might break down—and be typographically untidy—at the tops and bottoms of the pages. You might end the first page with *dans* and start the next one with *hort-*. In the garden: not very approachable, though I wonder. Readers can get used to anything."

"They do in Joyce." Shahid.

"Not least in Eliot, who does the police in different voices. All that lingo. All those lingoes." I am reminding, not chiding, him.

I think we have aired a genuine problem, requiring minute calibrations of type to page and across grammar and sense. What on earth had I been talking about in France? No wonder he hauled off at me; but it was a good idea in the abstract. I consoled myself with that thought, shelving it. I am thinking now of Raymond Roussel, the wealthy literary dilettante who would charter a steamboat to go and see a certain place (India, say), but restrict himself to a distant view of the Indian shore, at once, having seen it, returning to Paris, where he wrote his novels, always finding the exact center—harder than it sounds (you count syllables)—and installing there a pun facing both ways, say *moule*, meaning both mold and mussel. Formalist fanatic, he believed in grids and symmetries. I recommend him to them, for *New Impressions of Africa* and *The Dust of Suns*: books to linger over, continents to peep at and then hasten away from. I keep trying, as ever, to widen their horizons, to get them away from the golden oldies that infest English departments, away from the mediocre but much ogled F. Scott Fitzgerald and wearisome Michener. Sally, I know, fights the fight against what she calls disdain without realizing that taste is based on it.

"Shall we then say we have agreed to differ?" Shahid asks in his almost yodeling Welsh accent, as if Oxford and Hyderabad have mated. "Are you getting away with it?"

"Sure," I tell him. "So are you. We have arrived at a technical problem more the bookbinder's than the author's. Perhaps the real problem lies with the eye. As one who's been proofing for weeks, I can only say the eyes do not have it. I wish they did. It's more a problem for the poet, the sort of thing Pound reveled in, spraying his Chinese hither and yon like an incontinent cat. Perhaps reading the Loeb Classics, for instance, with the Greek, say, on one page and the English opposite, isn't that far from what I had in mind. Ideally, of course, we would like to hear the one and have the other, as with a TV earpiece or at the United Nations: a near simultaneity akin to synesthesia. The edges of all synesthetic experiences overlap, don't they?"

"Just," he answers, getting recondite, "like the Bay of Begnal and the coast of Bangladesh, where the marshes swill about and the tigers roam. The halocline reaches far inland." Laughter because he said *Begnal* for *Bengal*: a prof.

End of meander. The others don't care. I see Sally eyeing us both, mostly because we "talk funny" and mistaking the "plummy" English accent for something else. Shahid and I have Anglo gush and swoop, constantly emphasizing certain words, but we never go so far as to produce "extraordinary" in several acts and crashing emphasis, as if we have said "ex-TROR-dnry." With some, the *TROR* is often quite loud and long drawn out, as if you have captured Ceylon while invading India.

"Ah," I say, "let us rescue our overroasted moutons from the stinking abyss of the chatterbox. I am often asked, not always in the most charitable spirit, if I am trying to form a political party of the dead, assembling those notorious right-wingers Byron, Stauffenberg, Jack the Ripper, Klaus Barbie, Doc Holliday, and Hitler, to name only some, for a new takeover. The last person to do so came from Paris, asking why I have often gone for ready-mades: larger-than-life characters with a paranoid streak. My answer is merely that they existed and that ready-mades save you a lot of work. Why grandees then? Only because they existed, were in the main a bad lot, enacting a regime of evil. This was the son of Jérôme Lindon, Beckett's first publisher, but he lacked his father's chutzpah; on being invited to spend the night in our disused caboose, with bed and refrigerator, he begged to use the phone and booked the next Air France to Paris. Home and beauty. The next guest was William Gass, stylist, who seems to have read himself to sleep with *Last Tango in Paris*. There's a missed connection here. I would no more scant the thick and prolific universe than I would ignore its villains. In other books I have written at length about my parents, my school days, my spouse, my uncles and aunts, swimming, flying, and painter and composer friends, most of these exemplary humans; but people don't ask about *them*. They want the low-down on the bad men. In this, I suppose, I am only doing what Latin American authors have done for years, amplifying the tyrants and dictators as the brutes of their own polity. I once heard that certain Latin American novelists had agreed, each, to write a novel about their own dictator; but only two, Carlos Fuentes and Julio Cortázar, a Mexican and an Argentine, went through with it, Cortázar's gift being the corpse of Eva Perón burgeoning mightily underground and polluting all of Latin America. I guess Roa Bastos the Paraguayan was never invited, or García Márquez; certainly the one's *I the Supreme* and the other's *Autumn of the Patriarch* fit in. As a child, I experienced Hitler's bombers, riding my bike to school each day and watching the sun come up in the north because Nazi bombers had unloaded overnight on the city of Sheffield only seven miles away. You tend to write about such things, setting up a short rope to the killer's neck. My main choice, after re-creating Stauffenberg, the most famous of some two dozen Hitler assassins, as a dead narrator, will be a novella about Hitler as a failed Vienna painter. Obsession? No doubt; but he's there, and I do not have to build him up from scratch before I set him in motion. I have long contemplated writing a novel about a character called Gravy, a sardonic and exuberant mimic who, dressed in all manner of drag, accompanies the action at the Antigua cricket ground. A tolerated clown. A beguiling fool. A wordless critic."

🖋 *Heroes*

Now Christina pipes up, lately of ancient history, at least until I saw her startling piece about a butcher's shop. "Isn't there something Carlylean in this preference for heroes or anti-heroes, counterheroes, whatever they are? Persons of conse-quence! If that phrase still has any merit. Wouldn't we all, unless we've become besotted with deaths of salesmen, rather write about, oh, Joan of Arc, Captain Scott, Helen of Troy, Flor-ence Nightingale, Palestrina? I don't think it's so much a matter of economy or hurry, but of the amount of humanity they stand for. Just look what the composers of modern opera fix upon! They want spectacular figures."

"I confess," I say, "to picking on the spectacular. Something vulgar in me, no doubt. But to begin with, I did base a trilogy on a wholly unknown, ignominious villager who achieved a bit of notoriety when he bricked up a girl on a housing estate. That, however, was early work. There were richer pickings elsewhere. You're right."

"Is it," she goes on, "the yearning to be in the big league, associated with movers and shakers, even if they're dead and gone? Artist's shorthand."

They agree, and contend among themselves, letting me overhear them. They have been still too long, so now they have a plenary indulgence, light-years from the undergraduate who complained, years ago, that what she wanted was something *structured* that told her exactly what we wanted of her, so she could tailor her work to our requirements! She didn't want to get the wrong idea. She wanted a Procrustean command. Here, however, around this cheap-looking vinyl table, her outstanding successors are thrashing out some of the aesthetics of modern prose, just the kind of thing that unnerves the conformists, patching together a methodology snaffled from Keats, De Quincey, Pater, Beckett, Borges, Cortázar, Nabokov, and who knows how many more, trying to figure out how much the modern or postmodern reader can take before losing patience.

I tell them the tale of how Borges came here years ago and called me up one evening just as I was settling down to watch a mediocre movie on TV. " 'Borges here, West. I have been with deans all day, and I am frightened. They are so academic.' I had dined with him the previous evening, chattering in English (I have no Spanglish) about De Quincey, a favorite of his, and the kennings in Anglo-Saxon epic poetry. I had watched his wavering hand sign books. Here he is again, asking if I will come and sit by him on the platform, not to interpret, but to repel boarders. I stir myself and change into what I consider formal wear. The huge crowd moved from room to room, he and I in the lead, and at last we settled. 'What is your favorite word?' He paused and tested a few against one another. 'Dim,' he said, and brought the house down, the initial trickle of laughter coming in like a tide as it bulged and spread. The whole evening was like that. He could not see my colleagues in the audience who shook their heads in amazement at my presence beside him. I put some questions to him, especially about Latin American literature, but also asked if he had really said *The Campbells are coming* as the coterie Campbell clattered toward his desk in the public library of Buenos Aires. He had. He had forced upon the reading public the mode of a blind man, and they had accepted his telegrams to posterity. The Taj Mahal of his self-esteem was booked full." I remember we spoke of the bad air that was *malaria,* his invention of such a word as *hrönir,* and his conviction that Cortázar was as silk-sandaled as an Argentine could be — no knives, no duels, no beef, but little rabbits being vomited up. We saw him off to bed and went home to read him. He was donnish whereas Nabokov was witty, contrasting students seen spooning as distinct from those seen forking. Our best conversation concerned writing about Nazis, impenitent ones at that, and how you had to pay for doing so. We talked of the protagonist in his *Deutsches Requiem,* a war criminal on the eve of execution, and a donnish, pedantic one at that, warily footnoted by both himself and his editor.

"*There's* a hero for Carlyle," I say to them, "the emeritus of dim. His mind worked up a whisper among the trumpets and the Evitas."

"Don't you remember? You said this wasn't a literary society anyway. Aren't you the same person anymore?" I should be accustomed to it, but I'm not, alert as I have become for the first signs of indignant accusation, ever quick to nip it in the bud. Thrash it out. They hear something, go away to brood on it for a month, and then, right in the middle of a discussion concerning Sarraute's desire to do away with "he said" and "Mathilde offered," the blowup. Have I become habituated to this generation's attention span? I doubt it, and, in spite of my announced "Please interrupt," I wonder at the sudden changes of tack they permit themselves, leaving connectedness far behind in the interests of a quick fix, a snappy answer, a *mot* they can quote on the day of execution. "Well, folks, believe it or not, this is that: I will not be back next year to pester and urge you. Some other taskmaster, -mistress, will be joining you in literary communion, and with luck I will be catching a few rays while thinking of you." They don't believe it, convinced as they are that a few words in the chair's ear will head me off at the pass, as once before. This time, though, I am really going, back to my first love, the sound of my own imagination.

"You really going?"

"Really. The paperwork is in."

"Who is going to plague us?"

"Well, I hope," I say, remembering an experience up in Michigan, "it won't be the local Elizabethan specialist." Once, for several years, I was that, not because I knew anything, but because I spoke with the right accent and so was qualified to preach the Bard to an audience of six hundred, three times a week, fixing (such is my perversity) on the bad plays (among others, of course). Leslie Howard or Ronald Colman would have done better. Never mind, I soon graduate to 512 and to the theme of the students' attention, their minds heaving out centrifugal felicities, asking about Roa Bastos even as we discuss Gide before getting to Calvino. The whirligig no longer deters me; I have become able at fielding all the balls aimed at me though sometimes the plurality and disarray of their talk sends me into a fit for order, promising them, if they would shut up for half an hour next week, to outline a Prosaics for the prose of our time. Fat hope. I may get away with a few allusions to the U.S.'s being a Hollywood or Nashville circus, rather than a let-tered one, but that is all. I flow with their impetus, recognizing I am here to help, not insisting too much on Flannery O'Con-nor's dictum that the student's taste should not be consulted while it's being formed. No, it should be consulted *before* it is formed.

Rosebud

So, then, why does writing, certainly of the sort practiced in this MFA enclave, come in a poor fourth or fifth, behind opera, say, and way behind the movies, the "theeartar," the ballet even, not to mention concertmeisters? A simple answer would be that, in a country reconciled to poor education, people nervous with English won't read it. The sophisticated audience is a hundred thousand. That's one version. Another is ten thousand (James Laughlin) while another (Amanda Vaill) is five thousand. It may be even fewer, unless literary sophisticates thrive on invisibility and can't be counted. A quick look at a best-seller list will elicit the response, Who are these people and what do they think they're doing? They're making money, of course, the Holy Grail to which the nation long ago dedicated itself amid the gross avalanche of advertising most of us submit to. Worse, there has come about a backlash against the novel, with C-Span 2 doing its best to fuse the concepts "book" and "nonfiction," as if fiction, after so long, has failed an important examination in profiteering. To see how alone you are, just try rehearsing a couple of tenets. One says that lexically ingenious combination of simple words into unprecedented phrases must never cease. The other says that language as a tool, an instrument, must always evolve; there must always be new ways of expressing and presenting, and in the right hands there usually are. Now wonder how many people, readers, are worrying about such stuff, and you know you're on the darkling plain with just a few like-minded folks. The world goes about its business without asking Joyce, Schönberg, Schnittke what they're up to. This is not to ogle gimmicks either, but to lament a lack of interest in innovation equivalent, I suppose, to interest in the miniaturization of the pacemaker or the use of stents in cardiology. "Why, then," I ask, regaining my lost voice from the inward ditties of this year and yesteryear, "did the French New Novel do better here than in France? Because, once the French realized it was a French thing, they got behind it. National pride in the arts caught up with innovation. Why, then, did it catch on here at all? Because it was French, a novelty. The French, though belatedly, see an intellectual advance; America sees a new toy."

"Are we doomed then?" Tim Mizelle, who speaks French and has read French books.

"No, we're privileged, if only we'll admit it to ourselves. We may even think we're the cutting edge. We're Sweeney Todds."

"Some novelists, maybe some poets," I go on, "begin work by drawing a small complex emblem, a bit like a *boutonnière,* in which all the ramifications of the book imply themselves. The book becomes a blowup of the miniature. Sarraute speaks of a sort of geometric figure, a circle with something heavy and small at its center, a stone statue, a pre-Columbian figure, which produces moving elements, as a stone thrown into water produces radiating circles. Hence her tropisms. Well, I sometimes think I can see a similar model when trying to sort out a poetics from the mess. I was just doodling here" (no blackboard in the room, no whiteboard, either). "Here, say, we find a rosette, which to the Greeks is a symbol of something as well as a rose. So, the part of it that's a sign implies the whole. The sign speaks to the senses, but the sign plus the ineffable speaks to the mind. Once you've split senses from mind, your world divides neatly into *en soi* and *pour soi,* on the one side the novel of things, on the other the novel of consciousness. The sad thing, for the Greeks and us, is that the two come apart, which is to regret that we no longer apprehend symbols in the round: to us they are highly specific counters or mystical tokens. Surely there was a time when, with both thrown together as the Greek verb *ballein* suggests, the concise majesty of all created things entered the mind at its most magical. What we call symbolism, therefore, has an elegiac sound because it indicates loss, severance, breach, recording our loss of—I purloin the phrase—magical realism. After all, the rash intimacies and cranky maneuvers of their gods were things they more or less took on trust; no wonder, then, that the Greeks, so prosaic and clinical in math, say, let their imaginations loose when viewing the stuff of every day. Eliot once called this kind of thing the dissociation of sensibility, which is when an ecumenical holism breaks down only to be retrieved in the published stories of someone like E. M. Forster (*The Celestial Omnibus*) and the unpublished ones of Walter Pater ('Gaston de Latour'). Two latter-day Greek holists. Are we dreaming when we think of coordinating the mind in such a way as to unify it, left hand and right hand helping each other out? A Julian Jaynes, suggesting that the voice of consciousness or something such evokes an older brain's overhearing of the gods, is on the right track. Religiosity may be old hat, but it certainly made more magical our apprehension of things the senses brought us. I think modern fiction at its best keeps trying to make consciousness whole again.

"What Eliot calls dissociation of sensibility evokes the state of affairs that Jaynes in *The Origin of Consciousness in the Breakdown of the Bicameral Mind* identifies as auditory hallucination; voices, of gods as in *The Iliad,* emerge in the brain's right hemisphere and tell people what to do when they're unable to think. Which leads me to conclude that, in olden days, 'before' consciousness, sensibility was holistic, not yet split up, and what the senses brought in came swathed in unified awareness. There was no symbolism then because there was no consciousness, no introspection."

Every Sentence an Experiment

🖎 In Camera

Today I sit, not quite writhing, but squirming left to right, after a surgeon's encounter with an abscess. Usually I sit rock-still, almost a parody of the *en soi* mentioned earlier, but now they watch my motion with mingled pity and distaste, especially as, against the odds, I try to simplify what we've been talking about. It comes out perhaps simpler than I intend, with an innocent once-upon-a-time prefixed to it. I should have gone to bed but am determined to prevail over the onrush of abstract ideas. "Once upon a time, when gods spoke directly to humans, the humans registered everything in a big mental wash, neither analyzing nor construing, but appreciatively open. Later, with the arrival of analytical thought, humans began separating thought from thing, analysis from sensibility. Which was when symbolism as we know it began, not least because it dawned on us that the world as it is and consciousness of the world as it is aren't the same thing."

"Are you in pain?"

"Ask Mercutio! Something about the wound's being no bigger than a barn door, but it will serve." Actually, this exemplifies my point: it feels worse than it is, worse than it looks. So much for our sensibilities. The pain, I tell myself, is all in the mind. Hippocrates doesn't help. After cutting, they shove a piece of gauze into the gap to keep it draining. Ah, a good topic to get off. Change the metaphor then.

"Much as Hitler got Germany handed to him on a plate, not through any coup d'état or popular vote, so do we use the attributes of the novel to upset the novel. He did democracy in by turning its attributes upon themselves. You needn't remember it; just recall its having passed through the fragrant sluices of your minds. In my experience, and this goes much beyond the novel, most writers have one big idea, or possibly two, and the second is often the opposite of the first. So, in one skull, you have the obedient novel of the conformist and the antinovel of the rebel. In the realm of nonfiction too, the rebel, unable to mutilate the facts in the expressionist's way, begins to tinker with the component parts of individual metaphors. There is always a niche in which, though you can't change the truth you're reporting, you can tinker with all manner of analogies—the things that thicken up the texture, especially if you are writing first person." I pause to squirm. They pause to watch. I look down, but see no patch of blood beneath me. I am pure. Must I go on? Is it going that badly? I hope not. Dave is still waiting for me to get to the nuts and bolts of his urbane novel. Last time I had my notes all ready, fresh and warm from the stithy, but now they've cooled a bit, don't come what the Irish call "leppin' fresh" from my painkiller-killed brain. Let *them* do it, then.

What happens now is what happened years ago when I taught Cortázar's *Hopscotch* to the parallel class in comp lit. They read the book, tolerated it, discussed it with their familiar blend of geniality and reserve, then plumped for the so-called Morelliana at the book's back, these the table talk of the failed novelist Morelli, who, unable to bring into being the novel he wants, theorizes brilliantly about it, concocting such terms as *liber fulguralis* (book of lightning), *theophany,* and *lo(co)gic,* as if Aristotle the guru of failed novelists had at last intervened, handing him a full professorship of writer's block. So now, the best and the brightest are treating Dave's novel in the same way, as if he has written it to a formula, say, adapting event and plot to a scheme out of Sarraute by Robbe-Grillet. Once again I have to come to terms with the prevalence of theory in academe, instantly favored, remorselessly and often obscurely applied, easier to deal with because it *explains* and seems to exempt the reader from tussles with taste. Only the most committed of writers refuse this gambit, knowing they have seen the flame, whereas too many of the people with degrees have poked about in the embers. Clearly, if you need to prevail, you have to lean the other way, insisting on the creative always, scanting theory as much as possible. In this, I am afraid, I, too, am guilty, too interested in the mind to let it float off. Anyway, now to work. I read Dave aloud:

> "A sister's face the color and texture of playground sand, cute, strong, and intelligent splattering all over Pepita, and a mother who didn't quite vanish or evaporate, but merely sublimated, leaving her padre intact but unkempt, morose and tepid, gnawed at Pepita's intestines — a pearl in progress, and progress.

"You can sometimes achieve surprise without extravagant imagery or bizarre combinations. See how *gnawed* brings the whole sentence to life, back to life? I detect a flavor here of Djuna Barnes, almost a defiant grammar culminating in itself, or in the question: What is this pearl? An egg? What do you think?"

"I almost liked it." Nomi. "What looks like an ablative absolute turns out not to be, which is a neat enough trompe l'oeil, a challenge to the reader's breath. I do get the feeling that he's left spaces blank and then goes around filling them in. *Unkempt, morose,* and *tepid* are pleasing enough, but then I wonder if he's worked enough at it. Could have been, oh, *blasé, slurred,* and *lustful.* Sorry, a suggestion only. Don't cut my head off."

"She's making a pointless point." Sally.

"She's trying to do what *I* do, sit in somebody else's skull." Myself.

"I don't know," Vince says as if intending a longer sentence than the one he comes up with, its cadences pointing more skyward than you want. "Seems to me that the design of the sentences spares him the need to outdo John Donne, say, or Joyce. If you get enough backward-looking into it, you can rest easy."

✍ Experiri

Dave's Nina Cuidado fictions, destined to compose a novel, remind me of Ben Jonson's humours, I'm not sure why. Perhaps it's Dave's willingness to amplify beyond the point of need. Jonson writes:

> I will have all my beds blown up, not stuft;
> Down is too hard; and then, mine oval room
> Fill'd with such pictures as Tiberius took
> From Elephantis, and dull Aretine
> But coldly imitated. Then, my glasses
> Cut in more subtle angles, to disperse
> And multiply the figures, as I walk . . .

He fills in a strong and simple outline with curious admissions. Dave just about provides the modern version: flatulent impromptu. They listen to page 2: "how the steam looked like a thick piece of steel wool come alive as it oozed out of pipes on tenements across her street and rose in great, rolling waves up from roofs into the gray roil of the Manhattan sky." I see a few conciliatory nods. "You see how gently he ascends to the image of steel wool, a substance that might have appealed to Jonson. The section as a whole takes off when he gets into two long paragraphs of poignant recognition as the narrator discovers everything he has ever done makes sense only in relation to Nina: *She laughed with her old smile, a beautiful catastrophe, at my plastic Congo, my transparent Africa of lonely, aching, white heat and white noise.* I think it works, partly because it may baffle, to begin with anyway, but then I wonder if it baffles enough, takes enough chances with the world of everyday things that overlaps somewhat with the everyday world of everyone else. He might achieve this effect by complicating the syntax more, catching us off guard.

"I mean it," I say. "Dave excels when he whips up a taxing rhythm. Perhaps plain characters survive quite well, thank you, if outfitted with a contrary rhythm. There's a jazz tune called 'John Somebody's Wife' whose wobbly glitch just about tells you she has a wooden leg and walks with sudden, regular lapses of the kneecap. Anybody know it? I'll look it up."

"Pepita's more vivid to me than Nina." Mark, being economical.

Agreements abounding. Dave doesn't seem to agree, but he keeps quiet, turning on them a look of unvindicated pique.

"Oh yes."

"He's in search of some nullity."

"His novel-to-be is."

I ask him to read the Pepita sentence aloud. He does, with especial emphasis that proves to us he's already seen the end of that sentence several times. He knows where it's going, whereas the unanticipating reader, perhaps not game for gulps of air, each within the previous one, is not going to be ready for *gnawed* and its suffixes. All the same, he reads it with conviction. He knows where it's headed in the paragraph, too. *Ars celare artem,* or please stuff your cheese-coated aluminum foil down the side of the cushion. Dave should always be crisp and use his rearview mirror.

From time to time I encourage them to see their work in an almost Dionysian way, at its most creative, trying to experiment in every sentence, not through wild excess but with tiny, almost covert touches that will transform a phrase. Be concise to begin with, I tell them, and then stretch it out like elastic, filling in all the spaces. "Tell yourselves you have been put on your mettle in every utterance, just to see what will happen. I think Dave does this now and then, holding back the salient verb almost like a frustrated German. He's right not to overdo this ploy, but he does do other things too, hence my comparison with the oft-maligned Jonson, a poet of the surface. Sometimes Dave's imagery comes from Woolworth's, other times from the witches' cauldron of his imagination. When he writes of 'my plastic Congo, my transparent Africa,' he is doing original work of the surface, but kept so concise we don't feel the need to expose it for what it is: a trope that perhaps can't stand investigation. Left thus, crammed up, though, it works, mainly for what it doesn't tell us; it offers an outline, suggestive perhaps—he won't fill in, maybe because he can't be bothered. With Pepita, though, he's working with material that's almost too swollen to fit, and so you get this wonderful sense of superplus—he's deploying a vision almost too much for the sentence it's in. I call that experimentation, experiment from the Latin *experiri,* meaning to try, test, prove, put to the test. That is what he does, proving his vision on our pulses, setting himself up within the frame of the sentence rather like a scientist executing an experiment in the lab. The whole idea of making this one as good as I can, and then the next one, has some appeal, especially if you can hide the workmanship so much that the reader responds to the audacity and the elegance without spotting the twists of technique. If this strikes you as too overt, too demanding, remember how prosaic and pedestrian one can be within the live wires of the sentence. Or, to change the figure, within the confines of one of those foreshortened, narrow swimming pools in which you swim against the mechanical tide; nothing exposes the awkward swimmer faster than one of those. So too the sentence, a narrow room in which to hang yourself. Watch how Nabokov deals with this, contriving to make each sentence somewhat different from its predecessor, even if only switching, say, from iambic to anapest measure.

"This means, then, each sentence becomes a challenge. You can almost always be saved by finding and using a stark, blunt word. For example, take the sentence *Potentially the operation was lethal,* which might easily become *He could have died during it.* Not a clever or fancy example, I admit, but you will never go far wrong if you add a leavening to your prose of such words as *slouch, brash, drone, snite, brusque,* and so forth. I am not disparaging Latin; indeed, to write *itchy eloquence* is fun because it gets the reader thinking and is certainly better than *the psoriasis of eloquence* or *eloquent psoriasis* (if you must). Perhaps there is a magical ratio for those of us who work in English and Latin-Greek (unlike Italians and Spaniards, say). It might be three to one: *turd, boor,* and *drivel* entitle you, maybe, to one *incalculable.* I am making this up as I go along. Say: *A boor's turd is incalculable drivel.* Never forget you are the heir of all those Greeks, Romans, and French who imposed themselves on the Anglo-Saxon of old; you are privy to at least two different kinds of languages, and lucky you. Remember how huge our language's dictionary is, and add to the list the monumental slang of American English. For the lexical opportunist, life becomes easy provided you really take advantage of the riches that crowd you in."

"Is there," Mark is wondering, "anything racist in all this. I don't really care, but I wonder if there isn't a long-standing prejudice against Romance languages, I mean on the part of the Anglo-Saxon speaker?"

"If you're an aesthete of language," I say, "no, I don't think so; but there's a delivery in cricket—a ball bowled in a certain way—called a Chinaman; and I always winced when South African friends said *bloody kaffir*. Yet to the question, Is there prejudice, I think the answer must be yes. We like to think our English, our American, is sharp and earthy, like a turnip rooted in sludge, see. You'd trust someone who talked like that, though he/she might be a monosyllable-toting rascal. Let the writer beware: *turnip* is good, but the Latin *rapum* isn't much worse, is it? Writing, you are at a fancy bazaar, and your only responsibilities are to read the dictionary and honor the oldest principle of all. What?"

"Tell the truth."

"No."

"Keep your eye on the lion."

"Not bad, but no."

"Don't be verbose."

"*Contrast.* Art goes to sleep without it, and so does the reader. Get this straight. You are not being journalists, scholars, or critics; you are writing art, high art if you like, and it has to be inviting as well as of a sufficient solidity (heavy enough!) to oust the world of every day. Don't aim low, any more than a boxer should. When somebody takes your best experimental sentences and recasts them all as simple declaratives beginning with *the,* give them a fight. There is one inexplicably popular autobiography with successive sentences all beginning *I.* Now that's not writing, it's doing the dishes in an Irish bog. It's almost as bad as—who's that guy?—William Trevor, who excluded Beckett from *The Oxford Book of Irish Short Stories* with the *Thirteen Texts for Nothing* staring him in the face through the stained-glass ogive in his rectum? Excuse me, now and then the cobra will come out and spit in someone's eye." I end by wandering off into that other art I envy so much, still harping on contrast. "If you listen at all to the most rapturous and metaphysical music of Olivier Messiaen, as distinct from his excursions into the vocal patterns of birds, you may hear behind the most exalted themes of divine accessibility and human yearning a snatch of an old earthy tune, leaking out from the numinous lattice: *When I grow too old to dream* (which I did not know you could get in French). Similarly, if you listen to the near-Wordsworthian music of Gerald Finzi, you will hear a refrain just as earthy, installed there to profane the main theme: *Baa baa, black sheep, have you any wool?* Amazing, isn't it, when these virtuosos bring the world together again for us (the thing and its name) in the manner of the Athenian Greeks?"

But I am alone with, at best, the apostles of Bach and Haydn. Mine isn't 512's music at all, nor are those contrasts real to them. They are much more attuned to the visual, and they hoot with helpless post-Magrittean laughter when I fish out a bookmark that is actually a letter from Steve Donatelli, a predecessor of theirs who, after ten years of teaching English at Harvard while conjuring up a PhD dissertation for Brown, went off to Singapore and now announces his imminent return in an envelope bearing a one-dollar stamp (Singapore currency). A blue car shines against a horizon dividing yellow from ocher. Atop it sits the familiar FOR HIRE sign. Above the car, introduced with a coiled, swerving uncial, it says TAXI, and I wonder at the need to say it at all.

"Is this Singapore thing an introductory course for foreigners?" I ask, but no one knows.

"What if it had said *This is not a taxi*?" Dimitri, whose Greek ancestors entitle him to *some*thing, although they would have good reason to parade their attractive alphabet in front of foreigners receiving envelopes.

"How to learn words fast," says Mark, giggling.

"It's not," murmurs Julia, "as if it were a word engraved on a sundial. Maybe if you combine the *Singapore* at the upper left of the stamp with *Taxi,* you get *Singapore Taxi.* But what's the difference between an American taxi in Singapore and one in Altoona?" I scour the stamp for quintessentially Singaporean details, but find none, unless it's a shadowy figure in the right front seat, suave driver leaning out.

✍ Talked Out

"You're in less pain." Vince.

"I have warmed to my subject, Vince. The heat in my head

exceeds that in my rear. The pain in my heart is less than that in my head. I have decided to let myself loose, my excuse being that the anesthesia's wearing off."

I get the feeling that, if I were to shut up, they would have a cocktail party on the spot; no booze, but lots of mental spirit. I once offered alcohol to a group of students in my bolt-hole, and most of them went to sleep, as did I one day out in the May sun with my back to a tree trunk, trying to teach. Once there was a distinguished visiting professor of art history, Battisti, whom we called Ciaou-Eugenio, at this very college, and he did a whole semester's teaching in two weeks so as not to be too long deprived of his beloved Italy. During those two weeks his wife read the philosopher Leibniz, on whom she was an expert. I am drifting off, away, to the tune of off-duty chatter that discerns a new release in me, a surrender to Percodan or whatever. *He is talked out.*

What a warm warble conversation can be! If they aren't talking literature, it must be scandal. Yes, he's only just arrived and he's screwing every girl in sight. It's the money. No, he's really strapped. His parents give him nothing. I don't like spinach, I can't abide it. And Canadians wear it for a full week. Yes, barbed wire shows up well in aerial photographs. Well, I won't go. Skanky. Brace. Anchorite. I'll get an A for that. You'll be lucky. It's art, remember. Fuck art, I need an A.

I sometimes feel like the person who, calling someone to dispel a muddle, gets into an even worse muddle that ends in a flurry of ill-couched apologies, and who barks into the mouthpiece a curt asperity not addressed to the other person at all, but rebuking his own muddle. Any stylist, I tell myself, knows a torment of the calling: an able student advancing yet best left alone so he/she won't crash into the razor wire of the profession where Himmler and his lean, spare, taut, thin, svelte greyhounds wait, or, less fiercely, the minimalist puritans who "edit" prose, or the lumpen-public who clamor for what's simple, plain, and anonymous. The writing style I propose is that of extreme awareness, since to write any other way is hardly to write (or be alive) at all. No ideas but in things is all very well, but from the seventeenth century on, the baroque mind has also wanted to acquaint itself with the mind that produced.

So with the arriving class of novelists each year, so-called. You ask if any of them has the indelible badge that begins with love of language, language's art and finesse, the impenitent uniqueness that some benefactor has honed and refined in a fit of altruistic despair. Who now, you wonder, having swum as far as fragrant print, needs further help? Well, none of those with media-hyped novels and expensive badly written promo for the Miramax movie to come. None of these certainly. Is there not, I find myself asking in a punitive dream, somewhere someone agonizing about life as an ordeal to be rejoiced in, just like Ralph Vaughan Williams, whose idea this was. Maybe I am deluded, but these dozen, sometimes more, are serious performers, on paper anyway. Don't be so tough on them, uncle.

They have heard rumors (English departments are rife with them because the rewards are so small), but they hardly credit them. He wouldn't walk out on us, would he? Well, he says he's devoted to the language, and that's all. He wants to go back to writing, of which he does quite a bit already, though he claims he can't write while teaching and, every year, can't wait for May to come, so he can resume, and deal with all the ideas that have been boiling around in his head since January. He only teaches one semester, anyway. They aren't exactly driving him. Maybe he isn't well. I've heard it said, honest. I know what I'm going to do, I'm going to apply elsewhere. He sure looked wobbly, he comes and goes. Yeah, he uses Givenchy, you can smell it a mile off, not cheap either. He can't be doing so bad. Something between a tyrant and an uncle, right? Yeah, he has a flame in his tail all right. Did you get all that stuff about this guy Johnson? Who the fuck was that? Drink to me only with thine eyes guy. Y'know. Classy. I wonder what he'll make of me when he gets to it.

"*Experiri*," I say. "See what you can do. Rest up with an aviation magazine. I think they recycle the same material all the time, but the soothing effect, as with almanacs, is great."

To Read

To *study* literature at all—as you might say you study someone's face or performance—is to encounter a host of voices liberated from the page; or so I find it. To study literature in the presence of others is to hear them too, liberated from the rigmaroles of, for instance, "I want you to read the collected Emily Dickinson over the weekend." (Such things happen all too often.) If this is to be lax, then so be it; let me be lax. Better that than what I call the sarcophagian mode of study, in which students like coffins eat the flesh of books. My own way, even with literature classes, has been to remain informal, to be on the alert for impromptu findings, *trouvailles* someone was too shy to utter, something written down for praise but never to grace a seminar room. Hence my willingness to be interrupted, or to go back and repeat something, or even to go after a concept repeatedly, like a terrier, until it gives up the ghost. This is casual teaching, at its least capable of introducing readers to evidence of the world: higgledy-piggledy, at random, a swarm of incompatible details with which any imagination is going to have to deal. Literature, I've always said, unless it's generic and abstract like Pär Lagerkvist or Turgenev, is a matter of details amassed. One vulgar way of registering it, apart from literary study, is to open both ears at a cocktail party and submit to the conflicted surf of chatter that surrounds without enlightening you. You can even glean some idea of it from the potential hubbub of MFA voices attuned to your sudden silences or lapses into painkiller doldrum. Without this, the student may persist in some platinum vacancy of grouped ideas from which recovery, qua creative artist, may well become impossible. I have often wondered what a slow, systematic reading would do to such a person if they addressed Kant, say, or Heidegger—I choose at random from *Being and Time*:

> Because of the kind of Being which is constituted by the *existentiale* of projection, Dasein is constantly "more" than it factually is, supposing that one might want to make an inventory of it as something-at-hand and list the contents of its Being, and supposing that one were able to do so. But Dasein is never more than it factually

is, for to its facticity its potentiality-for-Being belongs essentially.

Is this more or less fun to wallow in than something I composed not long ago as an attempt to mimic the bleakly mellifluous style of Maurice Blanchot?

On the littoral of an insentient nothing, she felt the ghost of an absence, one which, having been known, had moved as it were sideways, enabling other shades of meaning to thrive or, if not that, to assemble in meaningless, dead echelon above a Thames seascape whose contours evoked the barrens and the fires in the margins of the universe where, doting on the word "be," she roamed on weekends, cosmically loafing, as unable to die as to change the absurdity of absence into the absurdity at the hardly beating heart of absence. Always . . .

My idea was to inculcate rapture without making the meaning clear, although the rhythm almost suggests something beyond verbiage. One can have fun even while going bonkers. It is more substantial fun, however, to contemplate the eccentric savvy of Ludwig Wittgenstein's "The truth cannot be stated, and it cannot be whistled either," or his longer apparent paradoxes in the closing passage of *Über Gewissheit*:

I cannot with any seriousness think that I am dreaming while I sit here at my table and write. If a dreamer says *I am dreaming,* he is as wrong as if he said in his dream, *It is raining,* even though it is raining. Even if the rain suggested to his sleeping mind that he dream of rain.

We can save the reader from Kant or pseudo-Blanchot by invoking even something as bizarre as Joshua Lederberg's dictum on how to look for angels:

Unexpected line-structure, superimposed on the doppler broadened lines of, say, the 21 cm H microwave emission.

Coming from the Stanford School of Medicine (the genetics department), this has a certain allure, especially to me, who have written a novel about angels but, more importantly, have seen a UFO, which I will describe further on. The reader gets into home terrain with Henry Green's bleak sentence about love:

It is the horror we feel of ourselves, that is of being alone with ourselves, which draws us to love, but this love should happen only once, and never be repeated, if we have, as we should, learnt our lesson, which is that we are, all and each of us, always and always alone.

And beyond it in Joseph Conrad's poignant record of his first flight:

No, never anymore, lest its mysterious fascination, whose invisible wing had brushed my heart up there,

should change to unavailing regret in a man too old for
its glory.

Cap this with a characteristically backhanded Irish witticism,
and you have some idea of the linguistic spectrum a reader can
be exposed to:

> Is there an Irish equivalent for *mañana?*
> Yes, but it lacks the urgency of the Spanish.

A literary education, especially for someone creative, has to be a
synecdoche: a part taken for the whole, as does book reviewing.
Survey courses prove it, as do academic anthologies of other
kinds. There is just too much, and the amount increases daily,
which means that the whole idea of the well-versed person rel-
ishing the scope and texture, the evolution and pauses, of a literature goes by the board. It becomes increasingly impossible.
Enter sciolists and skimmers, or experts whose special topic becomes ever narrower. The student reader enters willy-nilly into
the dark night of the not-known, vainly struggling to make responses to work he/she has never read, judging the hidden part
of the iceberg in the light of the decreasing tip.

Of course, university courses can extend themselves to five
years, say, but there seems little social impetus for that. The
worthy and the unworthy mass of art and literature piles up,
sifted if at all by increasingly hard-pressed devotees. But who is
to deny a civilization its sap, the copious crescendo of response
to the human bind? Already, libraries have begun putting out
feelers to houses in the neighborhood, stacking books away

from the main building, making them harder to get to. I never concocted an eclectic syllabus for my course in comp lit without a pang for all I was neglecting; and managing to cover a certain amount of ground over ten years, say, did not make me feel much better. The student, then, must surely be acquainted only with writing at its most gracious, chosen by those who know, who are very few. It will not be long before creative writers (awful phrase) will end up repeating what they have never read. Heaven help us when we reach the point at which harassed, swamped students grazing the surface of literature will emulate poor Custer of the Little Big Horn, who, confronted with the sentence "*Léopold duc d'Autriche se mettit sur les plaines de Silésie*" (Leopold duke of Austria set up on the plains of Silesia), discovered therein a leopard, a duck, and an ostrich. Some flashy person will get by with a hasty triplet—myth reposes, hypothesis proposes, fiction poses—and go on to vacant, hapless glory as a full professor of knowingness even as MBAs overhaul the publishing profession into a branch of the stock market.

Anne of Cleves
Leering

Sally's Run

Usually, MFA students wait until the last moment to hand in next week's work, but not these people, who sometimes, out of huge confidence, pass it out in class well before the appointed day as if there's nothing more to do. It's perfect and hasn't so much been abandoned as brought to consummate conclusion. It takes guts to behave like that, and I am thinking of creating a medal—for mercy and heroism while under fire. "Wouldn't you like to take another week with it?" I ask, but they have washed the whole thing out of their minds. On they go, having created Africa, to give birth to Asia. Then, of course, the class gets to grips, with a full week or more in which to get picky, and the results are sometimes vivid. I think my comments in class are harsher than my after-the-event notes, which I type after so many complaints about my handwriting. It must be daunting to receive a dozen commentaries all at once.

Do they sulk? Hardly ever.

Do they fight? Sometimes, always orally.

Do they vow to improve? No. Prejudicially ecumenical.

Do they feel they have let themselves down? No, only me.

Do they go away and publish regardless? They do.

"What's up?" I ask in my cheery way as I confront their bristling, alert faces.

"*I'm* up," chirps Sally, who has just done her daily run from Athens to Marathon, but isn't anywhere near out of breath.

"Actually," I tell her, "you were up weeks ago; I've just been carting it around with me, hither and yon, giving it the test of time, which is what Carl Ruggles told an impromptu guest who found him making elbow clusters on the piano for a piece about 'The Strong Silent Sun.' If you don't mind, I'll begin with your beginning. Would *you* like to read it aloud? You'll have to get your feet wet one day, no matter how nerve-racking it is. There, you see, you can often identify a speaker by the way he mixes his metaphors." Several of these people wrote me a politic, agile letter asking to join the workshop, revealing their considerable credentials. Sally was one, but I don't seem to have her letter anymore. *Filed,* no doubt, and therefore lost.

"You tell me if I read it all wrong, then. I talk funny, as you know, and I never read American dialogue out loud, as you also know."

In fact, her opening paragraph, like the rest of the story, is fanatically superb. Where did she learn to write so well, with such confident lapidary brio, taking chances all the way? At Yale? Marathon? Running fast?

"On a midsummer afternoon," I begin, then stop: the title has prepossessed me, I explain. Something called "*Ich Liebe Dich and Other Lies Too Hideous to Utter*" has such a sagacious ring (evoking perhaps "For Esmé—with Love and Squalor"—that same expert insouciance with startling words); I like the angle the thing comes at and its sturdy sophistry. I resume, and read the first two paragraphs as if munching chocolate cake on a snowy afternoon:

> "On a midsummer afternoon I stood in a crowd that thundered and snapped like a Dionysian bonfire. Children ran in circles, flailing and falling, tearing at their Sunday clothes, snorting like pigs. A woman passed out carrots topped with moist and feathery greens, tomatoes and tepid lettuce heads from the well of her apron. A lunatic tried to sell invisible copies of *Assertio Sacramerborum Adversus Martinum Lutherum*. A man near me ate fire off a stick, then another man spat a geyser of foamy beer into his mouth. From the combustion of beer and flame rose a tremendous hiss and a splutter of thick smoke that smelled like last week's roadkill mixed with cheese. Then suddenly an unseen force clamped the whole thing down, lock, stock, and barrel, and we riveted our eyes (I mean literally—there was piercing metal—it hurt) to the scaffold.

Onto it stepped Thomas Cromwell, sausaged in a burlap sack with his legs emerging stickily and yellow as if they were braids on either side of a Valkyrie's head. If Henry had thought of it, he would have put Cromwell's penis on the block, but Henry's concept of cruelty was rather banal. At the time I couldn't suggest it; my English still wasn't quite on, and my sense of irony was nonexistent."

Silence: thunderstruck, assenting silence, with a few daunted smiles here and there. It isn't that I resent Sally's running; I don't. I used to run, myself, a mile in a circle in the basement with mostly Beethoven playing (it would be Bach or Schnittke now), and when I played professional cricket I kept in super-trim like a dervish. But, if she can write like this, should she ever be doing anything else? I read it again, even more slowly, breathing more efficiently, knowing that this is the way to elocute anything, time and again until it has engrossed the heart. I tell them that Diane Ackerman used to recite long passages, in German, from *The Notebooks of Malte Laurids Brigge,* not as a party piece but as a homage. Something about images of a man's death haunting him while he's alive.

"Do you think," I say wickedly, "there's any hope for the author of this story? Recommendations, please."

"Holy fucking shit," says Mark.

"*En français, s'il vous plaît?*"

"*Sacré foutu merde,*" he says, scrambling to oblige.

"Then we can pass on," I say. "Anything else?"

"You're kidding," says Last Lisa.

"Nothing but. It's a stunner, and it goes on stunning. I like especially the detail of the distant world she evokes, the unrelenting accuracy and sly focus of the whole. It seems to have come to birth intact, fully fledged. *A Story.* How did you do it, Sally?"

"In pain," she says, flushed.

There is not so much a chorus of praise as a skewed medley, with voices beginning to overlap until a crescendo develops of mingled praise and clinical tribute. Yeah, the way she pins it all down in the very opening. I don't care about Dionysian, but I do about the bonfire. Best thing in that chunk is the pigs, the carrots, the greens, the tomatoes, the heads of lettuce, the apron well, the beer, the fire, roadkill, and the cheese. She's giving us the down-to-earth of every day. First-person narrator really opening up with steady surprise, she being in a weird sense more important even than the head and the block. It's an exercise in pell-mell narcissism. Vince, talking with an authority he doesn't always assume. "Well, you've all read it," I tell them, "what's the one thing that abides after you've put it down—I mean finished reading it? I must confess I found myself beguiled by—wait a moment while I find it—*her leafy smells: chamomile, yes, and walnut, birch, sassafras.* Same goes for *the calla lily curve.* I'm looking at style, but I do relish the circularity of the whole. How Narcissus-like." They go on about *Hannibal's oliphants,* noting the French origin, the Bosc pears, the men with heads like garlic cloves. I try again. "This is the self-destruction of an astute, acute phenomenologist way above her station. Anne of Cleves is ugly, ugsome. Take it or leave it. What's unusual, and I think adroitly contrived, is the way the woman behind the story exposes the woman who didn't know the ablative absolute."

✒ *Print*

Later that week, with Sally's story in my carry-on, I fly up to Buffalo to a conference at which several people will read and some, me included, discuss. One audience member makes a fool of himself, being a local author not asked to participate, so he invites himself into our company and bellows his displeasure. Afterward, Brad Morrow, editor of *Conjunctions,* easily the best international literary magazine, sits on a bed in the Holiday Inn and chews the fat. I hand him Sally's story, which he pops into his rucksack, and tell him how splendid we have found it. "Ready for print," I say, "without a word's being changed." Ironically, I end up in a Syracuse hospital, prey to acidosis, and miss a week of class; but when I at last return, I know that Morrow loved the story and will be writing an acceptance letter to Sally, who knows nothing about the deal. The next time she comes to class, she is clearly overwhelmed. The tears of ecstasy flow, only slightly provoked. "It isn't *this* easy," she groans, "it can't be." It usually isn't, but every now and then — and I devoutly wish it for all of them — along comes a work so carpentered and finished, so lexically original and so cleverly maneuvered, it simply falls into sweet-smelling print, no questions asked. The accomplice-catalyst in me is satisfied, but my eyes are blurring from some pill given me to curb the diabetes the hospital found.

In a letter, years later, recalling how, after class, the males repaired to a bar (according her "boy" privileges, enabling her to recall how Vince offered to break some fellow writer's skull with a bottle), Sally remembered sitting with a drink as she read the class's comments on this story. She looked up and caught the eye of a friendly literature professor, who then smiled at her smile and crossed the bar to kiss her. Would pleasure ever again be so full? Of course, but this was before she had any idea that her story was going into print. Was she granted boy privileges, I wondered, because she was such a sterling harrier?

When such things happen, you have to watch out for the others, who are bound to feel ousted, rebuked, shelved. It's only natural, so I spend extra time lauding the rest, but they're mature enough to know that Sally has cut off the examiner's head with a nonpareil piece. Her next work will probably be not as good, but she has without a doubt seen the flame and heard the elated birds who haunt the caravanserai with their flesh-eating, idyllic songs. You can't say *Welcome to the club,* but you can feel it, miserably hoping she will get into the right hands after beginning stellar. A book of her stories would be quite something to review. The problem will be to sustain that sharp, insinuative vision, ranging widely for almost Alban Berg–like material (*Wozzeck, Lulu,* and the rest), an outlandish chore she may well shrink from. Sally has tapped into the Zeitgeist and it is as if she has broken the German war code, Enigma, or discovered when

Admiral Yamamoto will be flying in a Betty on a routine trip, just so that a posse of Lockheed Lightnings can shoot him down. How often does it happen? A red belletristic day? Maybe after a good steak dinner whose juices hold long enough for that classic of yearning, the story written in one sitting, to happen even as you surrender to cramp, arthritis, and high blood pressure.

Next thing Sally has presented me with a glass wand, making me feel much like a witch doctor, though I have done nothing at all, and, as I wave the thing and utter blessings upon them all one by one around the rectangular table, I begin to wish I were somewhere else. All I've done is rubber-stamp her story, a thing all of her own doing. I look at those who have already performed, or at least been "up," the Lisas, Dave, and Mark, wondering if I detect the evil eye, the smoldering of pique, the prelude to an outburst, a *crise de cafard.* Not a bit of it; esprit de corps takes care of such emotions, but a few years hence it will not as they sink their teeth into their careers, or their pals, one eye on Gudrun Glum, the hot agent, the other on Queen Victoria.

Adam, just married, is pondering his lot, and Joe and First Lisa are getting hitched. I regret all these departures from their vows to Apollo, believing the artist is born to an abstracted, aloof life—*genus irritabile,* as the poet has it, whether the phrase be mistranslated into "irritable genius" (as often) or framed aright as "irritable sort." Sally and others inhale print and eat delight, but some, with something yet to prove (except Dave), have to heave the wheel and stay in fighting trim.

✒ *Futurity*

"What have you nice people," I ask, "got planned for your sixties?" Hysterical laughter from all. Oh, they will surely be dead by then. They hope so. "Will you pour a big midnight Scotch and sit by the shelf of your works, riffling through a preferred volume? Or will you spend your ill-gotten gain, if any, for a hit man from Altoona to wipe a rival off the map? Have you the stamina, the vanity, the guts, the self-esteem, the constant supposition that you are right and they are wrong? You'll need all that. The so-called literary life, about which lapsed writers compile anthologies of worshipful snippets, demands huge fortitude, especially if you determine not to write best-sellers, but to appeal to the literati. What will you do on an airplane when your seating companion asks you what you do and follows with *Best-sellers*? The best thing to do then is to list all the high-flown authors you know of, from Lispector and Cortázar to Pinget to Gracq to Gide. Don't explain who they are. Tell them, if you must, it's the passenger list. Travel first class if you can and knit fiercely all the way."

Perhaps they will become street-smart and haunt Manhattan, dressed in shiny black, their faces the white of mushrooms grown under violet lamps. I know none of them will pound away at a typewriter, because they don't do that even now, but rattle attentively on smart machines that parse, codify and paginate, even edit as they change from third person to first. I wish them ink and ribbons, but by then there will be no more typewriters, those workhorses, and Smith-Corona will have gone thrice bust, and even the most modest institutions will demand e-mail. In a word, will they get too smart? Of course they will, unable to remember a copy machine called Roneo that made wet duplicates and typewriter brushes that sported a white eraser on their tip and the little matte strips that were eraser tape. All their manuscripts will be flawless, assembled by a Japanese chip, while here and there a Luddite such as me will be banging his fingers into extinction and correcting strips of paper affixed with Elmer's Glue-All—the primitive, the barbarian, the redneck, actually incorporating the sullen correction process into his work as if he were a heart doctor or a brain surgeon, handling all with fastidious delicacy. I wish these things for them, not the streamlined perfectedness of their pages. I just wonder when humans will stop teaching grammar, with *vox populi* clamorous by the bonfires.

Coney Island Whitefish

... the empty condoms of our great loves float with no significance against one single, lasting thing—the stream.
—*Hemingway,* Green Hills of Africa

 Adrift

I am wondering if Vince Czyz's surname has been made palatable by the success of his brother Robert, otherwise the boxer Bobby Czyz, now retired and a forceful, fast-mouthed color commentator on Showtime. Wouldn't "Chezz" be better for an author, or even "Chess"? Mine own is an easy one, too common in fact (there are more writers called West than anything else: Rebecca, Anthony C., Anthony, Morris, Jessamyn, Nathanael). I consider myself qualified to offer advice. Like myself, Vince attended Columbia in comparative literature and developed an ease with foreign or even alien letters that stands him in good stead when coping with the antics of English 512. Smooth-faced, long-haired, he has a romantic air that shows in his cosmopolitan writing (he sometimes reminds me of globe-trotting Valéry Larbaud, a French lover of flight, recalled by T. S. Eliot for his *A.O. Barnabooth*). I feel some sympathy for Vince, I who at Columbia actually acquired the nickname of "lovely young Hamlet," believe it or not. I mean he is at ease with Genet and Melville. He speaks up with gentle finality and encourages anyone whose yearnings match his own, which is to say counterfictive in the manner of a young New Jersey taxi driver married to a Turk. I don't think the exotic has harmed him, although what I feel is his quixotic self has fenced long and hard with the boorocrats, often to his cost.

We are here today to discuss one of the component parts of his first fiction book, *Adrift in a Vanishing City*: not a story in a novel, but something, we have been warned, porous, semipermeable as the pig's membrane we used to fix to a thistle funnel in a school biology experiment. A saline solution leaked through, if I remember rightly. So does the banished everyday world leak into Vince's mutinies. The book has been to some fourteen editors, receiving generous readings but no offers, although the kindest letters explained to him the difficulty of reaching five thousand people with "this kind of hothouse writing, very lyrical, experimental, Joycean. . . . Too bad. He's very good." His prose isn't Joycean at all, and I think there must be a periscope somewhere for the twit who told him that. His own belief is that there are more than those five thousand refined readers out there, requiring only to be turned on. My own dread is that there are more MBAs in publishing nowadays than our putative five thousand (a Christly number anyway). Vince calls them "finely tuned" readers, and I applaud his spirit, the way his stories (if that) "*tend* . . . point into the distance, offering direction but not destination." They "overlap," he says, "are fragmented, with characters chasing each other from one story to another as well as through time." His "Fire from Heaven," which we are not contemplating today, "takes place centuries before Christ was born" (I wonder what size the audience was then). He speaks of their composing a constellation, "implying a shape edged in light rather than delineating a clear form, drifting aimlessly overhead rather than fixed in a particular corner of the sky." Perhaps he is composing a song of the sky.

To begin with, I mention my encounter, if such, with a UFO some years ago, while I was swimming, or rather treading water (a newly acquired skill). "It was huge, glossy, still, almost the shape of an ocarina, like the noses of two Boeing Stratocruisers chopped off and mated (this was the Boeing with the bar in its belly). Buff in color, it had no wings, but many square windows in a line, obviously a passenger vehicle of some kind. No sound. Perhaps it had arrived to become permanent, I thought, stuck at about three thousand feet. It bore no resemblance to any aircraft I had ever seen, and it seemed to be waiting."

"Have you told any scientists about this?" I *thought* Dave would chirp up. "Yes," I tell him, "and they frown at me. But I wrote an entire novel about the Milky Way some years ago, so maybe some of my images got through. In any case, I always thought it was empirically suspicious enough to call the object *unidentified,* implying unidentifiable; you didn't owe it more than that, even if you were a scientist."

"How did it leave?"

"At colossal speed, soundless, executing a vertical U-turn almost faster than the eye could trace. If I remember, I'll bring in the page I wrote about it. It was a lovely sight, so pure and inspectorial. You almost expected Danny Kaye to pop out of it." Now we get to Vince, who has agreeably been waiting.

Well, not quite; talk of a UFO has turned into some kind of literary foreplay, in which they chat at large about Vince's little essay on himself. I hear the neologism "cliterature" from someone and wonder if we are going to spend the next two hours astray. Once, I tell them, I heard the editor of a reputable paperback series exclaim to a roomful of people, apropos of somebody's advanced short story collection, "I can't stand *any* story that's more complicated than somebody saying Hi." I shudder. "You can see what kind of people Vince has been applying to, those who think literature has once and for all been fixed, not castrated though that might bear on it, but settled, ended. These dinosaurs infest the profession, as they do the professoriat."

"Is there any hope at all?" Vince talks up, impatient to get going, but willing to jaw.

At once I start to worry about people whose work I have not ferried to Buffalo to give to an editor friend; we should do far more for these people, we should not be so picky. *De gustibus* . . . It's no good arguing about taste. But it is, of course, and such writers as these, like as not, would resent being spoonfed into the quarterlies. Half the class, after all, has been in print quite often; but they thirst after the book, the seared-flesh, Chanel enamel stink that rises from the polished pages of the heaviest glossies.

✍ *Rapture*

"The problem with ecstatic or rapturous writers," I inauspiciously begin, "is this. If they make their experience — say, a private relationship to the universe — too far-fetched, they risk not communicating it at all. If they dilute it too much, they just lose it. Wordsworth and Blake get away with it, treading some middle route, whereas Shelley and sometimes Rilke don't. See, I am picking poets. Among prose writers, Teilhard de Chardin dilutes whereas Cioran doesn't; among novelists, Proust gets away with it and so does Lawrence Durrell, whereas Anaïs Nin and sometimes Pavese don't. It isn't easy, but Vince, because he not only does it repeatedly in several stories but also makes it the stock in trade of a complex book, manages to pull it off. What he seems to write about, in this and other stories, if they are indeed stories rather than, oh, floating ice pans of fastidious deliquescence, is ecstasy, when we are thrown out of our everyday selves by some ravishing experience we may not understand and therefore, by common standards cannot *eff.* Do you recall what I said about effing the ineffable? Most prose writers don't even think of it. Most prose writers don't even think, not even those who claim truth is stranger than fiction. *Nothing* is stranger than fiction, because fiction involves the whole imagination. Anyway, to get back to our moutons. Vince is more than a bit mystical; indeed, he searches for rapture, here in Budapest, gently remembering that those who prime their mind for the Holy Grail will usually find it, unless they end up with a collection of chamber pots. Did you know that the Romans cooked their lasagna in chamber pots? This juxtaposition of the sublime with the earthy he does rather well, as when he alludes to goatherds, or *my own tokens of everlasting devotion quoted to me by football players for weeks after,* or *a sloping Taygetus of garbage.* This is roughly equivalent to Proust's chalice of mashed potato. What he's really after, however, is to find mystery within mystery, to have experiences he cannot live without yet can't pin down. In this he recalls the André Breton of the novel *Nadja,* who speaks of life being deciphered like a cryptogram. Do read the illustrated *Nadja* when you've time."

Vince is interrupting, as required. "Do you recall the bit about wanting to become the mystery, even for a wing beat?"

"Otherwise," I answer, *"what is the point?* I was going to quote it actually."

"In case there are people urinating into the Danube?"

"Precisely, Vince. Sometimes a writer such as you can almost prevail through sheer metaphor, as Dylan Thomas often does. Your guy climbs the roof and projects his film onto the sky. Then you make your salient bid, specifying a stretch of cellophane that will or will not hold off a chill evening. It's a mild example, sure, but it shows what you can do. I think the petrified bloom held up by the wrought-iron stem is accurately done, as are the dormant lions, brought to dormancy by your own brand of animism. I sometimes wonder if you haven't come up with your own brand of visionary suggestiveness. I remember paragraphs that seem to have ragged edges, leaking away into Buda and Pest, or phrases that without all those dots appear to be doilies of the omitted. I mean, in the following, for example, you seem to be doing more than cityscape. *He be-*

comes the city, *she* becomes the city, even if—or because—she is the *belle dame sans merci:*

> "Sleep as distant as the memory of childhood I am no better off than a dead leaf, a discarded snapshot curling at the corners, swept end over end down deserted streets, the edges of cities even continents apart always the same near dawn-scattered bird twitters, shadows turning their slow pirouette into brick and stone, the same cold blue-of-drowned-lips appearing in the sky—and I wonder what, besides the brooding shape of Budapest, is silhouetted against reddish amber.

"Now, that's not your opening, but it might well be, with its key words—*dead leaf, curling at the corners, swept, edges of cities, dawn-scattered,* and so on. It is as if shredded maps occupy you most, transparencies and fringes, people whose identities do not have clear outlines, for themselves or others. Take Cortázar's *62: A Model Kit,* about an unnamed European city—Oslo, Paris, Barcelona. To one person it seems city A, to another city B, and so on, and the various misprisions of their setting help them mystify one another. In him, the surreal scatters and multiplies the photographable. You know what Neruda said of him? Anybody who doesn't read him is doomed. Not to read him is a serious invisible disease, as if somebody did not like peaches. In the end he would lose his hair. Exquisite kidding, of course, but he meant it. Read *We Love Glenda So Much.* Here, since I happen to

have it by me, is a Cortázaran city, akin maybe to one of
Chirico, but not exactly separate from Vince's 'unreal city' full
of dreams:

"You see, I am trying to prove how commodiously you fit into
contexts already in our heads."

"His so-called city," Mark says, "reminds me of a jigsaw
from which the little blebs that fit have been snipped off. Folk
cannot make the usual connections. The connections you *can*
make come from the metaphors."

"Which," says Dave, "is what those fourteen bloody publishers didn't like."

"Ah," I say, "they were reared on John Galsworthy and
Willa Cather and have never heard of Cortázar."

"I object, though, to the amount of surrender we have to
make to him. Taking him on trust." Who? Ended as fast as said.
Michael at triumphant speed.

"You want more leadership, more direction?" Me.

"Yes." It *is* Michael, ever in search of a lost leader.

"Valid enough," I say. "You wish he were more in charge of his narration and less, oh, wispy, filmy, uncoordinated. I must confess it doesn't bother me. I like my cities Calvino-ized. If it ain't baroque, don't fix it."

The cognoscenti smirk, and I shake my head, my mind now on how Eliot in his *Four Quartets* associates mystical experience—the veritable ineffable—with such tropes as garlic and sapphires in the mud, clotting the bedded axletree. "You have to deal with a heterogeneous world, as certain rabbis do. Otherwise you are as bland and smooth as taffy."

"He talks about visual alchemy. I appreciate that." First Lisa.

"Isn't the way he eats, the way he puts it all together," Joe asks, "exactly what his story does? He's a young man fumbling his fragments together, crudely to be sure; but I do believe his impromptu habits reflect his way of looking at the world. He eats hodgepodge." Joe beaming.

"Point well taken," I say. And the blues come into it as well. Who was it who said the blues are the outcries of a torn soul?" Nobody knows. "Let me read to you another piece of 'Budapest Blue,' just to see what it does to you when released from its page:

"I have gone every place we have ever been to see which has lost your shape, hoping to find you in the dawn-dusks along the steps that lead right into the river, in mist-draped evenings after the rain, in the deepest corners of the bars where we lost track of the flow of words and beer and the Milky Way, under the phosphorescent bridge where the old man watched, outside the iron-and-marble cafe where we first met, along the Roman wall where I exposed a whole roll of film to you.

"And then this:

"I understand the dolphin in you now, which is not a gray fish but a silver mammal, I understand why you left me here in the sluggishness of all this land, only the Danube to remind me, at my feet a mask whose plumes sprout a foot, the almond eyes lined with darkness, a mask exposing a mouth that could form the word that brings into being an irresistible emotion you've never felt rushing through you, the same mouth which holds the runaway river every dead sea lies in wait for.

"What he's doing is as overt as overt might be, a suggestion of the detritus amid which we all live, even though some of us have a keener sense of dislocation than Vince does. He's not entirely discombobulated, is he? He seems in reasonable control of his sentences compared to cummings, Joyce, Pound, Eliot, the dadaists, Faulkner even. Perhaps the problem is that of the Many versus the One, or the Fox versus the Hedgehog; what's tough is retaining all the disparate phenomena in the mind without losing our sense of order. Maybe there isn't any order at all and Vince is referring us to that fact. We have orderly minds within the chaos."

Julia

Who is this pale-faced, almost medieval-looking strawberry blond, suddenly contributing with diffident eloquence? I look at my class sheet. This is Julia, newcomer from Duke, someone who has actually read the old text *The Ancren Riwle,* about the day-to-day ways of nuns. I too read it, in the original, in my teens, and have quite recently gone back to it for ancient earthiness. "I can readily see," she starts, "how critics of the old school—ye Clifton Fadimans, say—would berate Vince for writing fancy, or for being sublime. I am not here to berate him, but only to suggest that, if imagery is to be on the surface, it should also sink roots from time to time, now and then sucking up something from the fifth level down, and we should have this reported to us with fanatical accuracy. The world is not a vague place, any more than the blades of grass in Kew Gardens, where Virginia Woolf knelt, were all the same. I do think one-third of Vince's imagery belongs in the easily acquired (and easily rejected) category and should be cut or made more specific. There is nothing tendentious in being accurate about the world. I allow myself inordinate liberties in my own writing, but I do labor for specificity, and I respect it when I find it."

She pauses graciously to mop with a square of handkerchief, at which juncture someone says, "That's enough."

Instead, she goes regally on, saying that, as Empson proposed, poetic imagery can and should lead to ambiguity. "Much of the joy of poetry, reading it as well as writing it, lies in the double entendres. I'm not sure, however, if narrative prose can get away with the same privilege. Now and then maybe, but in general it advances because its tendency is to lunge, is it not, because its images if any are propulsive. Torpedo, not puddle. In that case, it can afford to be woundingly specific, but not dilatory or ambivalent. *I* think Vince should go back to some of his easily acquired, cheaply rented tropes and razor them up a bit, so as to leave nobody in doubt about his blazing originality. If he doesn't, he'll vaguely please us, but he won't ever bring to bear the remorseless, intimate, unappeased gaze of the clinical inspector. I am pleading for a touch of the scanning electron microscope."

Again that unidentified voice. "I think you'd be better off in a dentist's office." Phlegm Snopes rides again.

"The money would be better," she says. "I agree."

Vince, a little stirred, is behaving well. He nods and gestures. He is going to speak. "OK," he says. "Well, I'll be fucked, I've been shot down."

"No," Julia tells him in her chastest voice, "you've been recalled to base." The voice of the turtle is heard. *Ex Elliott,* I murmur, for that is her name, *semper aliquid novi.* Julia will put the spike to all of us, like those Bulgarians cruising on London Bridge with poison-tipped umbrellas, looking for trouble.

"She's right," Mark says, "but Vince is right, too. It's often hard to attain sublimity, and you can't *always* couch it in exquisite detail. Sometimes, I do believe you have to do it in the raw, without getting too fussy. In his prose, there's a kind of Paul Bowlesy invitation, a constant thing inviting you out into the blank and open places, deserts or cities, but there's also the suggestion that, now and then, you can follow him *only* if the specificity of your expectations matches that of his best imagery. You have to be at least as qualified as Julia is, but you also have to have the common touch that allows the banality of certain movie actresses, say, into your world picture. You can't be too grainy; sometimes you need to be smooth and accept the golden oldies *as if* they had quotation marks around them."

"Quotation Marks," says someone. "Who've you been reading, Mark?"

Only himself, he answers, and his father's critical study of George Moore, about which I know.

"Jesus Christ, you two," I say, "you're on form today. You inhabit a domain of sparkling finitude."

"A domain of sparkling finitude," someone echoes.

"Write it down," I say. "I relinquish all rights to it."

Mark starts to laugh, joined by Michael, Dimitri, and Joe.

"And so," I begin, "the rest of you? Have we arrived at an important point? The heterogeneousness of imagery? Because, as Julia says, fictional prose has to advance, some of its imagery can get away with being smoothish, familiar, just so long as it's moving us forward—and, of course, if it's smoothing us toward somewhere it can get away with being familiar. Because it's familiar, it will speed us along. Instance: when Proust is eager to creep from one social scene to another, he keeps us within a familiar stream of images, but when he wants us to dawdle and schmooze with him, he talks science, which I imagine slows us all up, unless it's a bromide about the universe as an expanding plum pudding."

The highfalutin chat has topped them off. They have agreed and want to move away. Only Dimitri and Ed feel inclined to comment, and they do so pithily, without censure.

"Vince's a kind of midnight cowboy." Dimitri.

"His dreams have peculiar narrative force, more than what he recounts as events." Ed.

I shall promote them both to chief oneiricist. Julia's opening salvo has impressed them all, even Mark, who takes all good literature seriously. Vince tells us he has done almost half of his first draft, other story titles to be "Overhead, like Orion," "The Night Crawler," and "The Northwest Passage: A Portolano." "It doesn't take much," I tell them, "to offend the reactionaries. You don't have to be outrageous or flamboyant, only a teeny bit out of the usual. That was why my book on swimming, *Out of My Depths,* never got reviewed in one newspaper. A certain reviewer had looked at it and tucked into it the message 'Too eccentric.' It got put away, I heard, never to be seen again, except underwater. Thank goodness things improve. Next time it will be *In Deep.* Such people like literature fixed, final, as in O. Henry. The formula must not change. It's the kind of obtuseness John Hawkes argued against all the time. It's the mercantile approach. Why, there are Johnny-come-latelies in publishing now, as there were not in the sixties, who talk blithely of a 25 percent profit, whereas the house of Gallimard in Paris counts itself lucky to squeeze out 3. Above all, runs this slimy message: Do not challenge the reader with a long sentence, an unusual word, a passage of interiority. Writing for such people is to eat the recipe, not the meal."

"So?" Michael, raising head and hand.

"So stick to your guns. Write your heart out and tell yourself that, without luck, you're nowhere anyway."

"We're gamblers." Mark, mock-cringing.

"Good ones," I answer. "Highwaymen."

"Contemplatives," Julia says "How the hell—well, never mind. I'll end up teaching English."

"We should start a restaurant," Nomi says, "and wait tables. Readings at night."

"This *is* a restaurant," I say. "Look at the debris."

Mine Own Executioner

A Suit of Sables

I am enjoying them. They are putting up with me. At least that's how I feel about it. I was never on the receiving end, never took a single course in "creative writing," though many in literature. Each is someone's child, fostered and nursed and raised. The thought is almost stunning me. Know their faces, I tell myself, you will never know their bodies. Illuminate them as the Athenian Greeks did. Last Lisa has a Scandinavian tinge, acute blue eyes multiplied by glasses, fair complexion and blond hair, always a look of triumphant candor, which she deserves. For being always late, she has become a clear, definite icon, whereas the other Lisa, lanky and long-haired, with the diffident face of a searching animal, registers much without uttering it, but once launched will become almost giddy with sheer interest in her own theme. Of these two, the first is the more scholarly, the second the *maudite.* Mark, with a big ovoid head, might double for Eric von Stroheim, given a monocle and a thicker neck; I must remember his lineage, Welsh-German, and treasure his impetuous control. He is Dylan Thomas conscripted into the Wehrmacht and he lives on Black Moshannon Mountain. Dave might well have come out of Nigel Balchin's psychological thriller *Mine Own Executioner,* with the face of a boffin or backroom boy, intent and intense, spanning many worlds, all of which he wants to enter. He is a chubbier Kafka. Sally looks Cornish or Celtic, dark with a jovial smile that disguises her cavorting brains. I linger, wanly, with the thought that these, and the rest, have been entrusted to me, have entrusted themselves for grooming. Had I been similarly entrusted at their age, I would have panicked; instead, I was left much to my own devices except for a weekly tutorial, at which I read essays and so came to think of essay writing as something natural as breathing, whereas fiction is always the grand launch into the puzzling *swanroad,* as the Anglo-Saxons called the sky.

I test myself with comments typed in earlier years at the bottom of final pages:

Trim, controlled, and winningly paced, it seems to stop short quite often, the narrator unwilling to expose more of herself when we are on the point of wanting to know her fully. The piece or chapter works well on the level of reportage, but it could do more, weaving us into the teller's psychology and background much more. You are a camera, but you could be a stethoscope too.

Clearly, I didn't want to go on writing any more of this. Here's another:

> Enterprising. I wish you'd said more of these things or things like them, in class. Your opening voluntary is brisk and fetching, but it suffers from the component parts' being sometimes grammatically incompatible, and it would have fared better if you'd grouped things more plausibly, not straining the semicolon to the utmost. It might have worked better if you'd done three or four opening paras, each a catalog sentence. As it is, your reader sometimes doesn't know which construction persists or has been gone back to. A sprightly, audacious effort nonetheless.

I call that a noetic shrug, stiffing the syntactical steel wool within. My third foray is comparably critical:

> Some of this qua prose verges on eloquence, and that is welcome. Some of it, however, is rather drab—as parts of all letters are. Until you settle down, decide if this is a correspondence, or Letters Of, we won't know how to judge, but it's clear you have the flair to bring it off, provided you create the requisite fresco of interacting letter writers. So, it's a beginning. Now try a quartet or

a trio. I suppose actual letters would fit into this se-
quence, but you'd have to assert yourself against them.
A good reason, therefore, to write all letters with a view
to publication!

God help them, these recipients already lost in the penumbra
of the past-punitive. I could complain like a colleague of Syd-
ney Smith in the *Edinburgh Review,* whose plaint Smith summed
up as follows: "Damn the Solar System—Bad Light; planets
too distant—pestered with comets—feeble contrivance; could
do better myself."

But to be so, do so, is the worst kind of stale; better to lose
those absent faces and fix on these so that, adieus in bloom, they
will never go away or be masked by abstruse commentary from
one with better things to do. We are more like a club than anything, exclusive perhaps, certainly obsessed, and a better club-
room we could have—say, a US Airways Club, with whining
jets and semipalatial chairs. But I dream: we need these hard
seats, this vinyl table as yet unetched, this semidefunct air conditioner, the ghoulish parade of puzzled faces that peer in
before passing by. Here, not being part of literature, we go to literature the more readily, and that is enough.

In one of those torturous flash-forwards I see them in later
years, wizened and crabbed, all set up for an afternoon of cantankerous recidivism, their youth blown, their prime shot,
their only hope a rerun of *Spartacus,* well past the halfway point
and still not established, piecing their lives together year after
year while waiting for the destroyer of delight to let the ax fall.
No more of that. I swap its profane humanism for something

more mechanical they have not expected of me — I produce an empty box of Barbara's Fruit Juice Sweetened Animal Crackers got up in the shape of a little cardboard lunch pail and gradually peel it apart, reducing three dimensions into two, flattening the flanges and corners until I have before me what, if you look at it from the unprinted side, resembles two squat beings side by side with letter-box slots for mouths.

"Behold a *development,*" I tell them. "One of the wonderful things about fiction, nonfiction too for that matter, is that you can construct this kind of thing, with some market-wise circumspection of course, and then make it have three dimensions. Doesn't Forster in his *Aspects of the Novel,* a primer of the ancient approach, talk about round and flat characters? The trick is to find out what you've written: flat or round, and then to add the third D. An even cruder version of this maneuver is to lay out a bedsheet, flattening it with your palm, and then reach under it with a stub of pencil — the kind of thing Beckett's Molloy uses — and set it upright like an Iwo Jima flag, creating a shallow tent. It makes a world of difference. Here." I skim the cardboard development over the shiny table to them and watch them trying to fit it back together again with no evident joy. They do not, I regret to say, share my pleasure in toys, maps, models, replicas, hopeless homuncules, and I decide never to show them my model of the O.K. Corral, with the various shooters lined up correctly and sundry lookers-on stationed in more or less the right places — a toy without which I might have become muddled while tracking Doc Holliday through successive reenactments of the twenty-second shootout. No, I decide, they aren't ready for such funky stuff, nor for

(something much older) my collages of Colonel von Stauffenberg done in silver paper, with all his mutilations carefully depicted. At least, I always knew which hand he'd lost, which eye;
it's no use getting halfway through a novel and discovering you
have it wrong, although nowadays with a computer you can
put such matters aright. They don't know that after fifty pages

*Black-and-white version
of West's Stauffenberg
watercolor*

of that novel, because I'd misconstrued something in German,
I had to quit and start over, having assumed Stauffenberg was
hanged on July 20, 1944. He was shot in the courtyard of the
Bendlerstrasse, by truck light, but I did get my own back by installing him as dead narrator who restaged his own execution at
the end, to the amazement of many readers.

✒ Point of View

No: I tell them after all, and their somewhat academic response seems to be, "What? You got it wrong! You're not the flawless researcher we always thought you were. If *you* can nod, just imagine what *we* can get up to." So I tax them with something else: the hypothesis of how to present a highborn German with fair English, thinking in German but writing it all down in an English of my own. How would they do that? Dead end, except for Mark, who thrives on such conundrums. "You don't want to be judged on your German," he observes. "No fear," I say. "Well," he answers, "you write your best English and let the reader figure it all out. I wonder what one does when this German decides to use English."

"You give him his own English."

"Even when narrating, as distinct from talking?"

"You weave it in. It's a first-person novel in which I the novelist have to insinuate myself, and my supposed good English, past his reasonably colloquial German. There are undulations, you might say, but mainly he talks my lingo. Perhaps that's the novel's flaw. I don't know. Only the English complained!"

Already they are into such problems, although an extra problem for them would be a novel written in good old American English, which Stauffenberg couldn't think or speak. Now that would be a snag, to be sure. His English, like that of the diplomat Adam von Trott zu Solz, a former Rhodes scholar, was of the English variety, BBC English, public school, very producedly correct. It's an acute problem, afflicting such writers as Juan Goytisolo, Carlos Fuentes, and Mario Vargas Llosa, among

the ones I know, all of them highly educated in the English fashion and given to exaggerated refinement, Fuentes especially as
he also writes in English a long way from Spanglish. Such talk
amuses them, perhaps because they recognize a problem not
theirs, which immigrants had better address as best they can. We
do, memorializing Nabokov's Cambridge and Huxley's Oxford.

"It doesn't exactly apply to you guys," I tell them, "but I
have noticed how much American first novelists fix on the
same world, the same social hoops, the same dry rub of class
against class, race against race, whereas the world of literature
intervenes rather little. They are more street-smart than they
are book-smart, which may not be a bad thing; but remember
Malraux's dictum that art derives from art. You then get what I
often see, reading a batch of first novels as I sometimes do, the
same old same-old, with little chance of individuality, written
in the same sort of purged, starched language. These new novels overlap more than they don't, and this may be why American readers remember nothing, certainly of fiction. As Eric von
Stroheim says, if you have produced a decent work of art in
Paris, France remembers you forever; in America, you always
have to repeat your successes as if the nation is besotted with
the new, the modish, the novelty."

"Those who forget history," Joe says, "are condemned to
deplete it."

"That'll do, Joe. I mean, that's good to be getting on with.
I'm not trying to silence you!"

"Behold the tabula rasa," Mark adds.

"Here, listen to this," I say as I fish in my pocket for a slip of
paper. "There's always some Uriah Heep of the Rialto pecking

away at normal speech: *the poetical pyrotechnics that pass for style these days.* These zombies build ever anew, say the same thing always, mainly because they're prose invalids loathing the able-bodied they see striding by and leaving them in the dust."

Sally says something with a mincing motion of the lips.

She goes unheeded. Anne of Cleves becomes Anne Boleyn.

"No hope for us, then." Christina has a woeful look. "MFA et cetera. We might as well have embarked on doctorates, just to be sure of something."

"It's good for us writers," I tell them, "but I'm not sure it's going to get *you* launched. In the old days there were no MBAs in the way of the MFAs. You have a real point, but I have a sudden vision of you all 'making it' by thirty."

They look stunned, having always assumed they would prevail and shocked that anyone would raise the specter of their failing. Or have I misunderstood completely and are they mesmerized by my suddenly revealed vision of them in golden chairs, the darlings of periodicals that ostensibly devote themselves to books and literature? A memory stirs from my undergraduate days, when I joined something called the Poetry Circle, without the merest hope of becoming poet or peasant; I just wanted to be alongside others practicing the same art or discipline. In other words, I did it for art's sake, that phantasmal pipe dream. At most I hoped to publish a poem here and there, so perhaps I was soon infected by selling a poem to *World Review* in my teens or by the yielded-to temptation to edit an undergraduate literary magazine. Something was stirring, obviously, but with small thought of reward. I soon grew out of my innocent aestheticism, but not altogether; I can still be found, in my oldest gardening clothes, at the midnight hour, typing something for the sake of doing it, just to have the result on hand, without showing it to anyone. If you become wholly commercial, as the publishing industry now prefers, you have lost something guileless and Promethean, rather like those who, says Neruda, don't read Cortázar and will die of it.

I look at them again, serious aspirants all who perhaps haven't quite twigged the fact that what ultimately counts is performance, the creation over time of a body of work that holds up and is worth studying in the round. I do not yet see in their faces the prospect of hard work, when the rear end aches and the hand cramps, though to some of them this world of acceptance or rejection isn't wholly unknown. Perhaps they have already decided, some of them, that private amateur circulation is the best way to go—old Soviet *samizdat,* when you made your own copies in secret at the machine, or Elizabethan patronage, which required you to please your patron and be content with a small press run. If the hard slog they put in for me is any indication, they will succeed several times over, at least in the sense they will end up with a deep sense of having written something they can be proud of, never mind who says what.

Meanwhile, setting these pious hopes aside, I respond to their demands, when they ask me to talk about point of view, maybe the most requested topic of all, from the sometimes almost crippled first person to the godlike assurance of the third. You should always have good reason, I tell them, to settle for anything but the third, which confers on you enormous range and scope. I am not of the school that says a piece incorporating a child's view should be written in a child's restricted language.

Any verbally adroit third person can get across the child's version of things, from "crabbily aloof" to "blithe euphoria." Verisimilitude has little to do with it; after all, a child's world is not exactly an unknown quantity, and the problem will always be to eschew the clichés of it, not to make the child more real. Lifting up the slices of toast on a plate in a mood of Long John Silver curiosity isn't that hard to get across, and the third person does it in a trice while the literal child, penned up in a small vocabulary, has a hard time eluding the status of cardboard cutout. The first-person vivid present has special uses, as here, but it will in the long run trap you, make you want more overview, more scope for complex speculation. In the beginnings of the novel, Asmodé, a little lame devil, lifted off the roofs of houses so as to peep at the goings-on within, not far from a more recent image in the movie *L.A. Confidential,* in which Danny DeVito, equally small if not lame, edits a scandal glossy called *Hush-Hush.* He peeps, he tells, he photographs, he blackmails. And his reporting, even if camouflaged as "This reporter" or "Yours truly," exercises the same privileges as Asmodé or Henry James at his all-inclusive grandest. I promise to deliver some advice sheets I concocted long ago; asked to publish them, I declined, but copies have floated around, no doubt corrupting all who find them. All they will glean is that I think of the novel as a rather active essay spawned by imagination and can think of little that won't go into its loose bagginess. I was always more interested in prose, of all kinds, than in so-called plot, although the concordant imaginary incidents of plotting interest me more and more.

"Some of your novels are very long," says Mark. "One in particular. They seem to use small type, but that doesn't disguise the sheer length. Is it true that a novel is never finished, only abandoned? It's certainly true of my own."

Of which, I know there are already five, awaiting a sympathetic eye and ear. Mark has staying power, so once the great day dawns he will have a cache of novels to deliver to the world, say ten years' worth, which is somewhat encouraging, though not as encouraging as an instant sale of the first.

"I don't think so," I tell him, "if you know what you're doing. If you plan at all, you will have a notion of the green light toward which you steer. I must confess, however, I do like the idea of the Unfinished Symphony, or novel, *designed* to be unfinished, in all its incompleteness omitting nothing because the author has figured out the totality beforehand."

"You have just one book of short stories," says First Lisa.

"Yes," I answer, "I have short story attacks every five years. I'm having one right now. I used to say, every novel I plan turns into a short story, and vice versa. You can see how any attempt to second-guess myself misfires!"

"What about some pointers?" Julia, almost whispering as if the word had uncommon pornographic heft.

"Oh," I say, "there's always the pointer that Sally gave me. The wand. Seriously, didn't Plato in the *Timaeus* jaw on about how the past and the future are human fabrications transferred to the eternal essence? Only 'is,' he claimed, could be properly used. Odd to find him so up-to-date, so à la mode. We are like a fly caught in a dusting mop being drawn over the surface of

some painting. I can see that and enjoy it. Even more seriously, if
you dare out-serious Plato, I think there's a connection between
the third-person teller and verbs, so that you might have, as
first-person narrator, a rather straightforward person, almost a
sculptural minimalist, and then, built into the scheme, a much
prissier, fancier person who's given the chance to report various
doings, among them the fact that *Uncle Toby went to the toilet,* which
this prissy observer, intent on his own vocabulary, reports as follows: *Uncle Toby then repaired to the outhouse.* Thus you have a distinctive third person buried within a first-person narrative. Of course,
third-person narrators tend to indulge, if that's the word, in uncommon verbs, almost as if presuming to omniscience were an
intellectual act of some hubris. Try it, work it out. Put one mode
inside the other and see what happens. I mean, you wouldn't
do it the other way, install first person in third: much too obvious although we all resort to it at times because it's just so
damned convenient. Then I think of Beckett, who takes this
thing blithely, demonstrating that the mind is less an instrument than a place, a porous place into which anything might
swim. Therefore, he seems to assume, all narratorial modes
other than first are arrant contrivances, spurious and fake; the
spectacle, the sound, of a mind talking to itself, narrating to itself, as it were the scenario of someone chatting to his shrink
(which is the foundation of all Beckettian telling) with an open
mind, no restrictions, no formulas. He cannot bear anything else
because to him nothing is more tragic than the agon of the mind
explaining what went on. You can get any amount of performa-
tive bravura out of him, but this fondness for first will survive,

perhaps because it's the most honest way of telling, as poets have tended to find out—the poet is usually the speaker, at least in what we might call romantic poems. Notice how, when Beckett resorts to third, his vocabulary becomes more Latinate, more Greek, and the syllables in each word pile up, as if, in a whirl of jussive authority, he reserves the right to become highfalutin, exposing the true badge of authority. Am I making sense?"

No answer, but ballpoints are gliding.

"There is something else I call the voice of unique identification, and it comes from Dickens, who even through caricature, manages to make his speakers, and narrators, sound different. Just imagine, away from the Barkises and the Sam Wellers for a moment, how among the routine talkers in a novel a certain other voice, mind, would stand out because he happened to be made to say at some point, in answer to such a question as *Was he quiet?* Answer: *He spoke with styptic restraint.* Unless shaving, and with styptic pencil stanching the seep of innocent blood, nobody talks like that, but in novels, which are for the eye rather than the ear, they might. What I'm trying to get across is the malleability of the verbal medium. It really will obey if you make it do so, and sometimes when it runs away with you, it will toss up marvels. Be alert to it, to its manifold miracles. Why, only today, as I in all barbaric innocence read my horoscope in the paper, I found *Today, a new occupation is eminent,* which means *imminent* of course; now all I need is a character to get it wrong and say the one to mean the other. I rather like it, when what's distinguished becomes what's next. My *Roget* contains a Buddhist monk called a *bronze.*"

"What about character, please?" Ed Desautels piping up after a long silence of inspissated thought.

"Nabokov said it is a compositional resource, like imagery, and I agree with him, except that quite a few of my so-called characters have come from history, are larger-than-life, monsters sometimes, ready-mades I can do things with. Only the other day I hear from Juan Goytisolo, still not having quit Marrakech for Paris, agreeing that ready-mades confer upon us an enormous amount of creative freedom. If you happen to be interested in evil, as I am, you will find in history as many monsters as you need. So, as far as characters go, I am stealing images from the rival dimension even if only to deform them further. Enough. Time to hurl you out into the world of bourgeois sanity."

But someone asks about rhythm, and I postpone the question to next time, or even later. "I am the son of a concert pianist and am rather peculiar in this—I play in riffs and cadenzas. Ask me then about voice and tone, too. Some writers are writers of voice mainly—Beckett and Thomas Wolfe—while others—Dickens and Nabokov—deal with tone. It all has to do with dominant voice: the dominant ones are the monotonous tragedians, the adaptable ones are precursors of the rainbow, insisting on the deliciousness of human variety."

Out they go, then pausing in the hallway to argue fiercely, while others hang on for office hour, in which, because I mostly say things just as useful to others, I let all stay and listen, except by special request. Three hours of this and I will be ready to sleep.

✍ *Sez Who?*

The semester advances; I lose count of how many times we have met, even of how many pieces of work I still have to see. Clearly, there will be too many for the remaining sessions, so either we'll have extra meetings or we'll do two each time. What I dread, even though the room is always available, is extending the three to four hours. It always happens this way. Suddenly there's a bulge and we have more work to talk about because a number of them have come to the boil around the same time (the old hands usually go first). At the same time, perhaps because our wheels have become warm from running, we have more to talk about in the realm of theory. Perhaps I have truly woken up, or do I scent somehow the halfway point, the downhill run, the coming into view of the day on which I can devote myself to writing all over again? Which means, of course, my last hurrah. I feel like Mr. Chips, rehearsing his good-byes, anxious not to leave until I have imparted every scrap of experience, every wrinkle known to literary souls. It is going to be the same old squeeze followed by an open-ended walk into the twilight zone.

So off I go again, remembering and guessing. "Beware of a certain approach to dialogue that renders the whole thing complete, with a lovely shape, indeed the beginning, middle, and end we have learned, in discussions of plot, not to present in that order or not to have at all. Chop things off, so that the reader feels a certain amount of unexpended attentive energy that must be transferred to the next dialogue. Or, and here's the advantage, this unexpended anticipation will drive the plot or action instead of the dialogue. It will have been detoured to urge us from scene to scene. If you do it all through, 'axchanges' I call it rather than 'exchanges,' you may end up with a book that has a perpetual leaning-forward attitude and seems almost in a hurry to end without ever quite explaining what's been going on. You may even end up telling yourself this is the one device you don't want to be without, as if you were a foreigner in the U.S.A. and someone told you the one expression you will always need is 'all set'—you need only say this on all occasions to achieve the patina of normality."

Vince begins to say something that Christina interrupts only to have Nomi burst in with something that ends in "foster the illusion." Often a phrase will set me off, but not this one. We are having a genuine hiatus. They think he's finally dried up. I think I will tell them about the loneliness, the fabled loneliness, of the writing life, which I have never felt. It has ever been as if I am thirsting to play the piano and can at last get to it at midnight, in the dead silence of the sleep zone. Instead, I tell them about vows to Apollo and the sacredness of the quiet in which, if they are lucky, they write. It is a gift to the mind from the universe, evocative of those blank airless spaces in which nothing can be heard. I realize I am refurbishing Pascal's aphorism about the silence in the gulfs: "The eternal silence in these infinite spaces terrifies me." Yes, well, be grateful for it too and pray that your readers will have the luxury of reading you in a comparable hush. Down the table at the far end, Adam seems on the verge of coming back to life; he smiles, flushes a little, but then subsides into Pascalian dormancy. I tell them that, contrary to myth, at the writers' colonies, Yaddo and such, it is the poets who get up early and go to work, whereas the novelists, with far to go, lie slugabed till noon. Perhaps this will drag him out, but not today; he is keeping his own counsel, so maybe he didn't get enough sleep.

Why aren't they writing more?

How dare they slumber without having done their stint for the day?

If, by the day before our meeting, there is nothing in the coffee room in the box labeled 512, I know I will have to chase into my store of literary wisdom or give them a lecture on something unusual. But I lecture in 570, and they have most of them heard me. So I give them a version of Dora Carrington's credo: "When I feel low, I write in order to feel better. When I feel better, I go on writing because I feel better. She painted un-dulant forms almost as if she had read some such book as D'Arcy Wentworth Thompson's *On Growth and Form.* The thing," I keep telling them, "is to do it for its own sake. You will in all probability never meet in person or by mail more than a frac-tion of those who enjoy your work. And, if you are at all a con-noisseur of airports, you will end up wondering whatever happened to literature; what *was* it, was it ever read in stage-coaches or schooners? Avoid everything," I say, getting Becket-tian, "and then you will be pure. Never refer to a dream as a dream; mask it as a nervous breakdown or a butterfly hunt. Re-member that form will always accommodate the mess. Poorly written dialogue lies there on the page like little worms waiting to be punished. We have nothing to say, not really, so we make things up. Books distract the mind from itself. The more you correct, the more you have to perfect. Life is a series of interruptions. Nature works only with animals and asteroids; the cosmic machine doesn't work on the human level; nature devours people. American life extends between the lie detector and the electric chair."

I watch the tail end of their note taking. They think I am giving advice, whereas I am merely exercising the muscle in my brain suet that compresses, right or wrong. I go on.

"Introduce people who yesterday did not exist. Flaubert and Dreiser are very far apart. At least I hope they are. As da Vinci used to tell his painting students, watch a splotch move, then paint the movement. Plotting is sculpture, dialogue is archery. The first sentence in a story has to be a bear trap. Fully inhabit your narrator. Weak verbs are buried, like land mines that won't go off. Make a plot and float your style into it." If these are ingots, Zeus help me. If they are the germs of fictions, heaven keep me from writing them. My exercise is over. I watch Michael keep record, switching from single space to double space in a reporter's spiral-bound notebook. I love the story of his time at the university TV station, when they finally cajoled him from trying to run things as if WPSX were a snazzy hotel. He is better off in the wasteland of the empty page, dreaming of the elegant Nacional Hotel along the Malécon in old Habana, where Meyer Lansky used to stay.

"Is it true," Mark says in off-duty mood, having drunk enough aphorisms for one day, "that France made you a chevalier?"

"In the old days," I tell him, "you got a horse as well—if

you didn't have one already, that is. *Vive la France.* You know the tag about prophets never being honored in their own country."

"Will you *do* dialogue?" Someone plaintive.

"Yes."

"Or we could read Ivy Compton-Burnett instead." Mark sprucing up his dialogue.

"Indeed, Mark." Don't they ever talk to one another? The semester, I am saying to myself, begins in snow, ends with blazing Sol in May: a crash course in the universal.

The Uses of Words

Heraldry

Am I a river to my people? Hardly: more like a ruined spigot, leaking sultry memories nobody can count on. Today we are to examine Julia's "Uncle's Nephew," a hefty wad of typescript I find benignly eccentric, yet full of high spirits, as if she had imbibed something of Gertrude Stein and Thomas Bernhard. What I like about her work is the air it has of being a translation from some freakish foreign language, for some words of which — actions, states of mind, unprecedented moves of the body — there is just no English.

The class ruffles its papers, looks up, unprepared to speak. They have sniffed something bizarre and wait for me to OK it, as if I were some inspector general. "Julia's today," I announce, "in full cry. I'll read to you from soon after the beginning. I want you to describe the prose. Page 5, about halfway down:

> "And when I was fat and jolly, Uncle used to dandle me until I could stand it no more. I could use a good dandling now, always in need of a good dandling in fact, but alas, Nuncle is too old for dandling, but not too old to hook my neck with his cane-handle and draw me to his breast. I cannot remember when this gesture originated, or rather I can. It began in the summery deep when wigging duties began. My wigging duties began at the solemn age of nine when mange and dyes left Nuncle with a stubbly scalp of scabs. The light, bat-fruit yellow, gobbed in the orchard outside where giddy, I brachiated as fleeing bursts of purplish blackbirds punctuated my progress from tree to tree. Hundreds fled each tree. And as I paused to inspect a batch of shriveled nestlings, Nuncle hobbled out under the pear branches and settled like an odalisque onto his chaise longue, sending billows of pollen into the bright damp. The porch column behind him murmured its rich marrow of bees, muffling Uncle's caws, so when I finally swung down to him with a gargantuan blossom, his eyes were galled grapes."

They have been laughing, cordially enough, and now they get to grips, wringing the juice from it, remarking the weird use of language, the unapologetic eccentricity of the narrator, the ebullient proprietary sense of words—as if both things and words existed only for the convenience of the teller.

"Somewhat forced," Mark says, "although winning."

"She does it all through." Last Lisa has found something palatable. "It's like reading Lewis Carroll."

"Brave dandling," someone else says.

"Not much of that around nowadays," says First Lisa. "In writing, anyway."

Why, I think, this is stichomythia palace. Won't they ever speak at length about something?

"What," I ask, "do you make of Nuncle settling like an odalisque onto his chaise, *sending billows of pollen into the bright damp*? He may be too old for dandling, but he sure gets the pollen into the right place. He's a fertility rite in his own right. She may be twisting and contorting, but she does conjure up the bright promise of the pear orchard. No small thing. It's the kind of prose in which the words convey a sense of something going on, though you never quite know what, you are too busy learning and assimilating her lingo. I could quibble about *brachiated, gargantuan,* and *galled,* but I won't. We are in the presence of a verbal innovator, not quite the same as the Russian-touting Burgess of *A Clockwork Orange,* that oddly overrated homily, but daring and uncooperative. Go a couple of pages farther on and find this:

> "I jollify in the thickening night, howling outside this
> slit of window, and suddenly testicular, the jollity too is
> a lie.

"We are almost on the fringe of *slithy tove* land, which you may classify as nonsense, except that she never quite lapses into nonsense but keeps you hovering between—well, what? Perplexing physicality masked by recondite allusion? Think about it. The pissing out the window may entrance you—it's in the previous para—but what about the *Persian mute trundling tomes*? Almost anything could happen in the next sentence, which tells me she has created a texture amenably open, almost as if she were crafting an epic full of kennings such as *whaleroad*. I find this helpful because, certainly in prose, you tend to find the impending next sentence restrictive, by no means an open space in which anything might happen. There is something else that intensifies itself the farther you read: she tends to circle like a dog trying to sit down. Listen: . . . *under hived fluorescence*. Got it? *Some titbit with which to line my nest, some sweet pickling from days of yore, something silkened with the song of eunuchs, silkened with the sooty nights of sad eunuchs, nights herniated with moon, the nights for poor, poor eunuchs who piss through quills.* Watching out for catheterized eunuchs, you might miss the roundabout quality made evident by *silkened, eunuchs,* and *night.* Not much of a whirligig, but enough to spin neighboring words free from their connotations, down to their denotations, and even lower. What do you think?"

It is Julia herself who breaks the silence and the unwritten rule. "I confess to all the sins," she says with a voice quiet as a bleached whisper. "My biographical note—this was published—says *lives above actors*, which you can take as you wish. I am impenitently odd and have no intention of defending either me or my vexatious prose. I have only one question. Is there always enough going on to keep the reader awake?"

"*Packed*," I say. "As Keats says, every rift loaded with ore. You aren't kidding. They used to chide the young Dylan Thomas for writing obscure, clotted lines that could give rise to almost anything. There was always that touch of secretiveness. *Foster the light nor veil the manshaped moon, | Nor weather winds that blow not down the bone, | But strip the twelve-winded marrow from his circle.* . . . I used to quote that and then analyze it for the examiners. Julia doesn't go that far, but she does remind us of the foison of fiction. Anything can happen. The words will do as told. *In his nipple, the rajah hid a morning spoon with which to extirpate the molasses clod from the linoleum walls of his Mercator heart.* I just fudged that up. An enormous freedom awaits you if you will only see the end of the sentence as an abyss into which to leap. A bit farther on you find *Batna drowned herself in a fishpond live with saffron squiggles.* . . . Actually, this hesitation on the brink of obscurity slows up the reading a good deal, which gives you a chance to savor the interaction of her metaphors. Not bad. I think Julia is heeding my invitation to experiment in every sentence. In her language, things happen that have no everyday match. The *Arabian Nights* meets 'Jabberwocky.'

> ". . . just as the Duchess fell to beslobbering his head, the Duke flew foxlike from a bush and skewered the Dwarf, morsel that he was, on his sword, laughed, flung him into the birdbath (bath for peacock and emu) where the Duchess joined her lover on a bed of painted pebbles.

"Her cliff-hangers are kinetic. Her sentence patterns are not that clever, but the freight the sentences carry is almost always startling, which isn't a bad start. Well done, Julia. How long did it take you?" I think she says three years, and I believe her, but I am on the prowl now for others' responses. "What about, page 21, the raven's crissum around the fopmouth?"

✎ *Action*

At his most puckish, chin pointed like a playing-card spade, Joe comes to life with a long question in mind. It is possible to look at him and not realize, for the moment, that only a year ago he won the first Elmer Holmes Bobst Award for Emerging Writers, his judges at New York University Press the following: E. L. Doctorow, Denis Donoghue, Galway Kinnell, and Richard Sennett. Underweening we might call him, but his first book of stories, *Indentation,* remains garlanded, a piece of the main. "I very much enjoyed what you said about unexpended anticipation the other day, and I'm going to try it. What I want to ask about today bears on Julia's story to an extent. She devotes a good deal of her prose to madcap action, activity spawned out of seemingly nowhere, really an offshoot of verbal activity or, if you wish, a hyperactive brain. I mean this as a compliment. What's the cult of action in fiction? Why does it matter at all to have things happening, as distinct from characters meditating or having a meltdown? They get hyperactive, then have to have a yoga cleanse. Something like that. When we study literature, if we're lucky, we hear about the active life versus the contemplative one, which was an old medieval obsession, whose impact and appeal I can sympathize with. I know folk are supposed to get off their duff and DO things, otherwise they get the rubber room unless they're wealthy. What puzzles me is where this emphasis on the done, the busy, the hectic, comes from."

Roosting birds newly arrived from Key West occupy the faint, traffic-torn silence, and I realize that we have a quieter room than any up on campus. "Joe," I say, "it could have to do with the arrival of the novel as the camera of a new busy social class, the one that Jane Austen despisingly calls *trade*. Isn't there a character in Chaucer who seemed busier than he was? It could have to do with the contrast between the well-to-do, who can sit on their tushes, and the urgent busybody, Calvinistic rise of a whole commercial class. not the least of Asmodé's roles was to peep under the roof. So too with the kind of novel we call picaresque, which, sometimes fatiguing, is full of bustle, the pushiness of the picaro as he storms about in search of himself. Such a novel, parodied by the likes of Kingsley Amis, who offers a mild version involving a university lecturer like himself (who recoils at the sight of a pencil thrust through an orange), emphasizes the existential thrust, defining yourself in the world by your own efforts. Carving a scar on the universe, and if not on the universe, then on the blotter on your desk. The essence of the picaresque and the commercially agitated is energetic self-assertion. Let's call it a manner of being to which we all aspire, even the laziest such as I, even the busiest such as all of you. Some weakness or folly converts us from meditation to mayhem, as if only in action do we earn any kind of moral superiority. It sounds pointless, I agree, but we seem to have set up our society along those lines, scolding the layabout, the dreamer, Zeus knows why, and extolling the go-getter. So, in that sense, we prize the man of action and the fiction in which he goes after what he wants. It's surely a puritanical, capitalist idea. I wonder, if we had favored the other kind of life, would we have had literature at all, but only a plethora of haphazard, impotent daydreams? Morally speaking, then, we praise the busy novel because it suggests moral improvement. Do only the busy enter heaven?"

Joe is urging me on, though I seem to have put the argument in too extreme a form. At once I add something about the second law of thermodynamics, which guarantees a universe always running down. Therefore, we automatically laud whatever in it is always revving up. We remain in love with energy, no matter how crass its armature. More nods from Joe. Perhaps he is waiting for me to crash, having flown too high too recklessly.

"On to Julia," I tell them. "Maybe the energy in her prose is factitious, factitious!, and comes out of what—oh, lexical ebullience (I think so). We can only speculate what the texture of her writing would be like if it lacked that energy, that *sprezzatura*. A cortège of rancid mushrooms yearning for a jump-start? Notice how Proust stirs things up socially, at the soirée, the brothel, on the train, again and again to keep the bits and pieces in his fizzy drink on the move. He can't afford to have them settle to the bottom like lemonade powder. I think Joe has hit on something powerful and seditious that explains why most readers prefer a simple straightforward action tale that, while they sit still in the act of reading, speeds the mind up and puts it through a whole series of paces. Why, inert people can end up feeling active simply from having read *The Red Badge of Courage*, say. It's an illusion, of course, but who's to deny readers their dynamo or their anodyne? In any case, such readers, having memorized the line of action, and having found nothing in the prose, intend to throw the book away anyway, or leave it on the train for some other vicarious person to read. Railway reading it used to be called, and now it's airline or terminal. Who in his right mind would leave *Moby-Dick* on the seat? It has action, but much else too, which you'd probably want to keep by you forever. Sorry, I am beginning to bang on the ice like a polar bear hunting fish."

Joe seems to be turning an idea inside out. He is. "Has there ever been a time in which ostensibly action novels surfeited readers with meditation—what they really wanted all the time? Some would say that as soon as poetry of the non-epical variety invaded narration, the end was near. I'm not sure about that. Isn't it vital to have a scheme, a design, whether or not the characters are always active?"

"As distinct from a splurge, Joe?"

"Yes."

"I don't think so. I'm not sure that Julia's 'Uncle's Nephew' doesn't qualify as a splurge, but I treasure its verbal vitality. There's a scheme to it, maybe even an archetypal patter, never a hard thing to come by, from *Beowulf* to *Frankenstein,* from *King Lear* to *Waiting for Godot.* The exceptional fiction is the one that eschews pattern all the way, just as that forgotten book called *Gatsby* omits the letter *e.* It's still in the library, I believe. It's up to the individual writer to decide the pros and cons of (a) design and (b) action. To have both frees for textural experiment precisely those with no sense of style. Go ransack the Greeks if you want acute myths. Go ransack Holinshed if you want plot; Shakespeare did. If you want action, wind up your characters and let them go, frisky and eager. If you want to write medita-tion, get a good agent." I sense a black hole forming in the middle of the room, into which I, not Joe, have fallen, but it does lead me to another universe as stretched-out linguini.

Djinns

I am telling myself it's only reasonable that high-geared stu-dents will make pithy, concise comments rather than engage in sustained argument. They show a highly developed sense of their own thought, of its edifice, and they don't want it dis-turbed. Somewhat shy as well, even the experienced among them, they hang back a bit, then emerge with a groomed opin-ion, and leave it at that, having aired it for general consump-tion. I wonder what they will do when they have to give an hour's lecture, as some of them no doubt will. The power to sustain has not escaped them, not yet, but they will have to practice it somewhere, especially those who may not make it as writers, and these may actually be the best stylists in the class.

Such is one worry. Another is that I myself, reminiscing and recalling only to cast things in the present tense, will falsify what went on. Not in the round, no, but in the kind of excruci-ating detail an MFA seminar piles up. Clearly, some part of our proceedings has vanished: the throwaway remarks, the wise-cracks, even the cries of dismay or outrage. I feel like someone asserting that baby lions seem always to be saying *Ow, ow,* which of course they are not. Fortunately (and I cast this sentence in the immediate present), I have always had a memory, inherited from both parents, and improved by daily doses of blueberry juice, that superb antioxidant. I remember, reshape if I can, and set it down like an ancient of days, grateful to be remembering at all, and to retain that group portrait of the aspirants, all having a mission with the dictionary. So long as I have the gist, I tell myself, I said so much that I have said before, having changed my spots little in the last thirty years. Which makes of me either a scarecrow with a tape recording hidden among his rags or a monster of monotonous memory, an incessant clone of myself. The curve or trajectory of my thinking, expressed several times in collections of essays (and therefore consistent if I was to be any use as a commentator), runs from enigma to expressionist enigma, from De Quincey to Beckett, and from them to style as a response to the seething universe. My students could, can, easily compile a list of my bêtes noires and my heroes, neither of which need be rehearsed here, counting perhaps mainly on my facial expressions while speaking or answering. You can do wonders with a scowl or a brimming smile, or, if you are on your toes, a salient quotation.

"Back to Julia," I tell them, "I have to say that she wonderfully ignores the stock, the generic, the bald, with palpable steadiness achieving similarity of texture throughout. It's the unwobbling mode of presentation that will probably spawn a book. I wouldn't be surprised to see it one day."

Nods, pursed lips, a couple of judicial frowns greet that. The author herself disappears into her shell, having usurped the privilege by holding forth; now she vacates the scene, becomes a mere auditor, as if not wanting a grade at all. I always found her elusive and conclude that is the way she wants it, discounting attention as a gesture from other alchemists who had better mind their own business. She has a line, "gossamer socks of midnight blue, puce, Mars violet, rust, pumpkin, ocher, ghoulish lilac, rotten rose," to which I say Champion, but why stop at eight? She has no trouble with language or with (as I see it) extracting from literature its impenitent pomade, from which she fashions antiques of her own that she twists into attractive and uncouth shapes assignable only to her. Somebody at Duke must have lit the candle behind her visor, with some such injunction as "In this culture, you can no longer refer to a mouth organ without seeming frivolous."

Joe, our prizewinner, is eager for theory, of some kind anyway, whereas Julia, every bit as competent, works according to no theory at all, but continually disturbs our expectations of language until disturbance becomes her choice idiom. Why, you even get to know the kinds of references she will make next—Pertelote, Chauntecleer, djinn, Persian hen or mute, Zabaniyah Zamiyad, prince of eunuchs—and divine where she's coming from, possibly even conjuring up from your own reading compatible kindred allusions. Like the composer Varèse, she has experimented *before* beginning. She has discovered how writing will sometimes run away with you, not to get married, but to tempt you along, following each *trouvaille* with detective relish. I am happy to have read her, knowing that, as ever, she will vanish into a wimple of pink tissue paper, yet stably on course, although, of them all, the one most likely to get into trouble with pedestrian readers. So perhaps what I think her ingenious deference is a gathering of forces with which to confront the humdrum world, the Rialto of a new century in which publishing is the businessman's avocation. Whether or not she, a southerner, is typical of southern writing, I know not, but she certainly has a touch of finesse and earthy whimsy not much seen north of the Mason-Dixon Line. How easily she outpaces a work such as Speed Lamkin's *Tiger in the Garden,* once regarded as the cream of the writing in the Gothic seminars of the deep South.

Such is the pause that teaching gives: you get interested and want not to let go, eager to see how this comparative stranger develops, heading for Nabokov or Janet Frame, but you leave them in the butterfly net called the department, to be trapped and snagged in the years when they most need help, and you recognize there's a limit to your store of saws; you have your own consuming work to get on with, and so you recommend self-help instead, knowing how it stiffens the spine.

Whatever excuse you make for withdrawing, for taking the money and running, you are more like the man who enters the public toilet and emerges unknowingly trailing behind his shoe a twenty-foot streamer or train of toilet roll, which, if he is unlucky, he will transport at five hundred miles an hour to the other coast, no one having had the heart to warn him of what, behind him, is not gaining on him. We advance trammeled. If I were a southerner, I would want to write among the flowers and sniff the fragrant beaches, where it is perhaps easier to confront the horrors of the modern world. I flee winter anyway, on good advice, and admire the hibiscus growing wild along the street, the croaking parrots among the palms. I spend three hours a day just dreaming; in the North, in winter, I'd spend the same three hours asleep, in daunted hibernation. It is premature to recommend these maneuvers to my class; I might drive some of them into a frenzy just to get down there and stay, where, free on my balcony and able to breathe, as I was able in Tucson one entire winter, I envision the ghost of Wallace Stevens.

Tom Browne's
School Days

≋ Bronzed

Dimitri, with his angular good looks and lim-
ber, athletic frame, more like a young doctor than the dyed-
in-the-wool intellectual he really is, has asked me about my
affection for thick, eloquent prose, so I decide to tell the story of
Tom Browne's school days—a Tom Browne much earlier than
the Victorian one well known to schoolboys of my generation.
"Take a Londoner called Browne," I begin, "trap him in a room
somewhere in barbarous Yorkshire, cut him off from the stirring events of his own day, and watch how he performs. Here is
a Browne to keep in mind. He has studied classics at Oxford,
medicine at Montpellier, Padua, and Leiden. His prose is lyrical,
rhythmic, urgent, just about the first flowering of the baroque,

but his worldview is doctorly; he spends the years 1637 to 1682 as a provincial physician in Norwich, ever empirically attuned, but lost in a perfect trance, from which he emerges to see patients or to study a whale thrown up on the Norfolk coast, feed iron to an ostrich, or study ancient burial practice on the occasion of several dozen Roman funeral urns dug up near Norwich. He is amazing, rapt in superstition yet afloat in rhetoric, just about the first English prose writer exposing and exploring his own personality.

"He will appear from time to time in our reveries, a man no sooner lost than he finds himself in complex English, intent on dedication less to the sketchy empiricism of his time than to coddled prose. He personifies, along with Robert Burton, what I consider the literary opportunism that leads certain writers by the nose, compelling them to write down things that others would shrink from: unable to resist, not because the revealed truth is quaint or curious, but because what lures him on is the *esprit de l'escalier,* of which the French speak—finding the bon mot too late, as you leave the party and head downstairs. So Browne is really looking for a way of life that links the conciseness of phrasemaking with the elation of saying something— coming *up* with *something*—for the first time. In no time, after his first hundred phrases, he has a reputation quite apart from his doctoring: the tenant of a superstition he likes to keep outrageous. True, he explodes naive beliefs that Bacon cherished (coral is soft underwater, a salamander can live in fire), but such is not his main goal, oh no. He makes individual music from a countless stream of particulars amid which he knowledgeably cruises along.

"So then, you've met him, a mascot, a magus, a marvel. He comes to bear on a phrase of my own, never used but carried around with me in a little red book I devote to certain other treasures: *celibate gusto,* whose elegance I cherish, but whose ambiguity (the odd gusto of the celibate *or* the *reduced* gusto of such a one?) I worry about. I almost see him, nearly the advocate of his own Brownian motion, being tempted to use the phrase because—well, what? Because it gives a glimpse of life's plenty, onrushing and even concise, impetuous yet capable of being limned with sleek elegance—not prosaically but sleekly, suavely, demure.

"Suffice it to say that any discussion of Browne will range back and forward, examining such notions as *seize the day* and *gather ye rosebuds* and the romantic-Victorian notion of the hard gemlike flame with which you burn. When Browne ends a book, as he does *Urn-Burial,* with *Now since these dead bones,* he is writing consistently what Milton, in his prose, wrote only fitfully. Browne, I suggest, and some of those who followed him—Carlyle, De Quincey, Pater, and Ruskin—would have seen in the phrase *brand-new* much more than mere surface allusion but would have explored the blinding red or white of particles in motion, renewed and contained. It is perhaps worth pointing out that George Sampson, author of *The Concise Cambridge History of English Literature,* lauding Browne, waxes eloquent (in the war year of 1941), actually allowing himself an *o'er* as he pays tribute to *the most triumphant and sustained piece of sublime rhetoric to be found in prose literature.* Such is hardly the desired mode, as we learn from the prose of others. I have just gone through a shelf of those regrettable tomes called surveys, inflicted on an increasing number of un-lettered undergraduates; not one of them mentions Browne."

After the diligent note taking, faces will lift and my charges will (I trust) set about interrogating me; I grant that I have not so much met Dimitri's point as smothered it. But I haven't finished, not by any means. "Thank you for hearing me out for so long," I say. "Here's the rest of it. You may want Browne's dates: 1605 to 1682. The other Browne is a nineteenth-century schoolboy in a well-known boys' novel by Thomas Hughes. Along with Browne, you might just as plausibly set aforementioned Burton, author of *The Anatomy of Melancholy,* Lancelot Andrews for his sermons, and of course John Donne. Sumptuous prose flowered in those hectic days. Anyway, I picked Browne as my sample because I think he might be the best, along with Donne. What I'm driving at is the notion that the universe is a rich, complex, overwhelming place, utterly loaded with ingenuity and mystery. What a place to be abandoned in! Now, if it were not that, but a drab, stultifying place with little but mankind to stare at (all kinds of species not originating there at all), I could see the point of writing barely. It would be like being marooned in the gray convict world of *Alien*[3], a prison colony with limited imagination on tap. But it isn't. For some reason we've been gifted with imagination, some of us more than others, and it seems wasteful not to use it—the same with our power to calculate, to construe, to measure and design. It therefore strikes me as positively criminal to scant the huge harvest that the universe is by writing dullard sentences by the thousand, just so long as they don't demand much of anyone. I abominate waste, as you know, and relish expansive gift. If there is a God, wouldn't it be nice to have him saying, Well, at least you haven't betrayed your trust. Or something more articulate of course."

Seditious, clandestine cosmic laughter leaks into the room as if from one of the most sardonic novels of Wyndham Lewis.

"Beware," I tell them, "of pseudo-scholarly histories of aesthetic movements barely over, written by cretins who haven't read enough, just enough to squeeze by as experts on the postmodern." Dimitri is writing this down, too.

"I understand," he says, with an odd air of ownership, as if he has consulted the class; he will go onward to interview me and review *Terrestrials* with sympathetic gusto.

"So you can see," I add, "that in this case our old friend Roy Campbell would be saying *Not much sign of bit and snaffle, but plenty of bloody horse.* Our job, of course, is to provide both, curbing impetus and grandeur with grammar. It all comes down to not betraying the gifts you have been created with. If this lot is too windy for you, I'm going to *propound* some writerly advice from now on, bits and bobs that have come to me over the years, the abiding thing to which it all comes being *contrast.* Forgo contrast and you are as doomed as someone who hasn't read Cortázar. I'll look at my sheet of precepts and select carefully, now and then embellishing, and then I'll give you the complete list to do what you want with. After the mystical transits of Browne the country doctor, infatuated with miracles and the bizarre, come down to earth with me. All this was only an answer to Dimitri, who has been eyeing me for quite a while, as a former deputy sheriff of New Haven should."

"Has much work been done on Browne?" Mark seems to be fishing. "Quite a bit," I tell him. "Here, let me quote him at random: *That a Brock or Badger hath the legs of one side shorter than of the other, though an opinion perhaps not very ancient, is yet very generall; received not only by theorists and unexperienced beleevers, but assented unto by most who have the opportunity to behold and hunt them daily.* Ahem. How wonderful to read a sentence that really knows where it's going, almost a matter of sheer crescendo of cadence all the way from *Badger* to *hunt them daily.* My reading omits his quaint, optional spellings, always a source of extra savor. When he writes *That Molls are blinde and have no eyes,* he spells *moles* m-o-l-l and *blind* with an *e.* If being a doctor brings English this close to perfection, then let's educate more sawbones. Anything else occur to you?"

✎ Pound Foolish

They have detected the flame in my tail, expecting it to carry me even farther, and they are right. I have paused out of courtesy, and now I resume out of loyalty, becoming autobiographical, as they no doubt realize, eyes wide open, minds up for grabs, some of them smiling the smile of tolerant recognition. It isn't over yet, by Jove it isn't.

"Epiphany shoots through the green brain of a young boy attempting a difficult examination paper that confronts him with the topic: *Discuss Uniformity. Three Hours.*" It is as if I am deep in a fruitful dream, with at least one parent holding my hand, murmuring, *Show them, show.*

On I go, studying the reflexes of that young man. "How his mind reels," I tell them. "He knows he's doomed, that, no matter how well he has done on the Latin and French tests, this one will cream him. His mind empties out, until he recalls Miss Smith's unique advice on encountering the absurd. When you are stuck, do the impossible. He construes this as do something outlandish such as no other in the room will ever do. Don't go toward the topic, but sidle past it into something irresistible. So, after cudgeling his brain, he dreams up a book about gardens and puts nib to paper thus: *We do not know who or what he is, or where, but he is green amid green foliage, a green thought; a trickling spring encourages the growth of blue-green algae on the beard of this tribal elder.*

A hundred miles away, wondering how doomed he acts, Miss Smith feels proud of him. He hasn't quite, after Macbeth, chanted, "the multitudinous seas incarnadine, making the green one red," or risen to the Churchillian crack about a bridge in Spain: "Too many Basques in one exit." But he has tapped the world of the original, the outlandish, the grotesque, even, and senses, no matter how dimly, the layers of supposition a wordsmith can impose on the ordinary world. It is one of those Columbus-like discoveries that will keep him alert the rest of his days as he shifts from hack into fanatic.

"Soon after, being interviewed or viva-ed on his papers by an expert on Yeats, he babbles something amateurish yet zany about Tacitus and Caesar, goes blank when asked if he knows who Tully was. He should have known. Never mind. He has done well enough to be taken on, and he somehow knows this kind of stress will occupy his life, this almost continual quest for a phrase at least as good-looking as a movie actor. It will not always come, of course, and he will chide himself in later years for not always coming up with the mot juste, or the concisest way of putting anything, but he will have disturbed the context enough to get away with his attempt.

"There, it is done. Now he can go ruminating on the hairy chest of this woodland troll, dilating on the olive green of his face against the chlorophyll green of the trees. It may not be easy, but at least it moves along. As he pops nib into inkpot, he allows himself a fleeting backward glance at an opening sentence that might have made an impact. He has been present at the uncouth birth of the unusual.

"Much later, in the period he honors as that in which a certain Mandeville flower just kept on flowering, he remembers the woman who sat comfortably with the expert on Yeats so long ago and realizes she was Josephine Bennett, expert on Sir John Mandeville. What a long loop to throw around the world so late. From this Proustian conjunction, he knows, something unusual will ripen, even if not yet. By now he is accustomed to the extraordinary in all its guises, having committed enough of it, mostly without regret. Yes, he tells himself, that was a *trouvaille* long buried in the brain, surfacing at last either to be used or merely to be relished, and he rejoices. Not that he dreams the world is all of a piece, but he does relish the faint importunings of gracious overlap. In other words, the world, to him, who thinks he can call it together in prose, is less heterogeneous than people think it is. Then, refusing ever again to use a word as bubbly as *heterogeneous,* he fixes on *mixed* or *mixture.*" This emperor has no underwear.

"The phenomenon is well known, although not as common

as optimists think. For some reason, perhaps because his dream of designing airplanes has not come to pass, he has been present at something like Stravinsky's *Apollon Musagète,* nothing sweatily romantic about it. A Muse has flown up his nose and begun to peck away at his unresisting brain. After a while, training students, he will show them how that half-pencil rigged perpendicular under a sheet gives it contour and himself the occasion to ban sentences gone flat. Much later he will come to know that the art of prose is really one of sentences and that one should advance from sentence to sentence, experimenting with each, until the brand of so harsh a doctrine stunts the brain that spawned it, until the next time at least. By then, of course, he will know the rigors and strain of writing in his own way (he gets the pun all right), but by then is too set in his ways, with his spots and stripes, to change, when it is too late to stop."

If this has been a glimpse through a porthole, of an athlete stripping down to appraise himself in a cheval glass, or something glimpsed through a periscope on the high seas, they show no sign, but their comments are candid.

"So this," Mark intones, "is what it takes to make a stylist. It must be worth it."

"Just the off chance," I tell him and them, "of doing something that nobody else there is doing. They will come to hate you for doing it, being it, in the long run, at least those who can't do it or have moral prejudices against it, but you just go on spinning your cocoon of silk, as heedless as removed. You've just had the theory and practice of someone who learned how to recognize and choose his spots. All kinds of people will tell you there are moral, theological, logical, epistemological reasons for not doing it the way you do it, but you ignore them with a Promethean smile and get on with it, realizing what feels like not much later that you have assembled a career on it and, lord forgive the mark, induced others to go the same way. You guys, some of you."

Clearly the theory tempts some who lack the personal conviction. The appeal to identity tempts those who find the theory wanting. "*Theory,*" I say, shaking my head. "What a word. To the Greeks, *theoreo* meant 'to observe.' See how far it's come, how debased it is. We are always better off observing than theorizing, although it's theory and its acolytes that rule the roost in the English departments of today. By 2020 I wonder how many of those newfangled departments of English and social studies we shall have! Beware. Do the deed on paper, like an overscrupulous bum. Observe. Settle for an emanation from the personality. If you don't, if you write like everybody else, you will *be* everybody else."

"How do we get to that?"

"Beckett would have said by immersing yourselves in your own precious ipsissimosity. Drenched in selfhood. Never shrink from asking what does this particular work do to *me*? The anonymous-impersonal you have to leave to others, and that means taking risks, creating a vehicle, rather like Mark's usurpation of a Nazi bomber with unsynchronized engines, and becoming instantly recognizable by it. *Be prepared,* as Baden-Powell used to tell his Boy Scouts, to be charged with ego, superego, the infinite *I am.* You were not brought into this spotty world to pass muster; you were created so as to stand out in your creative difference. Hosts of well-meaning folk will try to talk you out of it, this commitment, but resist them; the universities are full of Procrusteans who will chop you off to fit. When you first thrill to hear someone compress a whole sentence into two words— *rueful jubilation*—emulate and so gather to yourselves a sublime power that many, secretly, will envy, and publicly decry. And please do not be lazy in your calling. That's enough, I think."

When you go off at the mouth thus, you perhaps expect eyes to shine, hearts to throb, but these excellent people settle for an aghast complicity. Now they recognize the ghost who has dogged their dreams. One of them is already losing the faith, I think, whispering the word *show-off,* so I sound anew. "And disdain whole cloth. Cut your rug from the unique fabric of your soul, so that, when you're gone, the wise will say you really lived. I am an Elizabethan. The French dub my style Rabelaisian marmalade."

≋ Parangs

"Sometimes," I begin to tell them, "suppress an aspect of your subject so as to reveal it later; readers may compare their guesses with the actual fact. Instead of editorializing, exemplify; let the reader construe your images and your selectivity. Don't neglect the irrelevant; bring it in now and then, to turn the reader's head away; then he or she will force it back with renewed interest in the world outside the story. Try not to streamline the world. Regard it as an almost ungraspable maze of unpredictable particulars. Ask if there's a greater degree of specificity than the one you're busy with. By the same token, now and then site a vague image amid fanatical precisions. Keep asking what the reader, with little prompting, can supply; then omit it. Make the reader an industrious accomplice. As narrator, don't be afraid to dominate or to intervene. Take complete charge of your work. A thoroughly dominant telling gives a greater illusion of a character's autonomy than a slack one does. Remember how first person traps you. Have your first-person narrator guess how a third person might tell things. Remember to say how things are done, how said, how responded to, and during what; don't halt, numb, stifle the simultaneous world while staging dialogue. Go for contrast all the way. Describing someone weeping, conjure up someone who'd *not* feel sympathetic. Use what lawyers call the best evidence unless adducing minor but immediate particulars. Enough of that. There's a handout for you. Just take what you want from that barrage of imperatives. If any of it speaks to you, use it. I'll do more of same another time, departing from the list to exemplify, which I suppose condemns you to writing down the examples. I'm sorry. I wish it were more structured. As they say, speaking of narrators, there's something seedy about Nick Carraway."

Nomi giggles, at which she is good, managing to impose a squirting gurgle on an almost Mandarin countenance. It would be humane to free them of the world's brute contagion, but I feel more counted upon to dip them into it, as if in castor oil. This very day I have encountered, in a serious TV show, a sentence that begins, "Buried two hundred years ago, British archaeologists claim to have..." Such things haunt me. They should know better. Why, even my doctor tells me to walk to the end of the longest line at the bank and thus, eventually, graduate as a non-type-A personality. Go at the speed of a chuck wagon, I hear: four miles an hour. I try, musing right in front of them on the usefulness or otherwise of reciting precepts in that bald way. Better, surely, to exemplify from texts, much as Plato pretended to do, with his amiable, sunny deceptions.

"Tell me, do you find such stuff useful? Or would you rather glean it from discussion? If I am the horse's mouth as distinct from the horse's ass, do you want to hear it from me, like that? There are undergraduates who would love to have such a list of requirements or inducements because, they'd expect, it would somehow match something they were to be examined on. Chances, however, would be that I'd examine them on something wholly inapposite—Milton's use of proper names, say, or periphrasis in Dickens. I gave up teaching undergrads when I realized I was teaching grammar, not creativity. I hear of one university that's trying to create a degree in creativity, lord help us, but the money's going to go to a new school of computer science, with a huge electric bill. Yes, Joe."

Joe likes structure because it gives him something to quarrel with. A sign of intelligence. Good. Sally agrees, and so does Vince. All very good, but I worry about them. Are they making a sufficient presence of themselves in the competition-ridden world? How on earth will they cope with publishers? I decide it isn't my duty, and promise to hit them another time with my Silver Age prosaics. One thing I discovered when teaching literature was that clever, able students had no vocabulary in which to express their opinions of modern writing. Not that they were inarticulate readers. Far from it. They simply had not been versed in literary history (expressionism, the absurd, the surreal) or in the jargon of such as Cortázar (the accomplice reader, for example) or the rarefied cant of Samuel Beckett, who proposes the *risus purus,* the laugh laughing at the laugh, which is to say a stance of utterly disabused contempt, and proffers such possible examples of it as "The mortal microcosm cannot forgive the relative immortality of the macrocosm." How deadly that word *relative.* For certain, I am not recommending anybody's jargon, but some of the concepts embezzled by the creative people of a certain time. They knew what they were doing and borrowed some words or phrases to limn what was going on in their work. In a way, what my MFAs are asking for is not precepts, but terminology: parangs or machetes with which to hack away the jungle surrounding intellectual endeavor. The answer, I believe, is to show them texts, let them try the terms on the text, and at the same time deduce precepts of their own from the actual reading. Talk about accomplice readers! Here they are, I say, entirely in your formative hands. You can do damage or good as you think fit. I ask them, from time to time, if it interests them to cull patterns from nature and adapt them to human purpose, as when I helped myself to the genetic alphabet in *Gala* and the structure of the Milky Way (incidentally making much of the so-called wobble in the code, which creates half a dozen ways of making a certain chemical, but only one of making another). Do stars seem to them to have human attributes?

"I mean something subjective, up to you," I say. "Not the stock appellations made up by the Arabs and Chinese, say, from the Seven Sisters for the Pleiades, Cygnus for the Swan, or Watling Street for the Milky Way. The imposition of an entire bestiary on the Milky Way," I say, "is one of the oddest things in astronomy. It reveals better than almost anything the human craving for resemblance and meaning. Sometime, scribble down the bits of astronomy you retain—Betelgeuse, Orion, Sagittarius, Lyra, Hercules, Southern Cross—and then research the names. You will be astonished by the inventive specificity of the naming, the references to the shoulder, say, or the thigh of certain identified animals. The whole university system, of course, trains you to look for meaning where, often, meaning is absent, so what you're looking at really is window dressing. More vivid, no doubt, than stars lettered and numbered, but in the end tendentious coziness. Stars are not like people, even though we speak of star nurseries, young stars, red giants, white dwarfs, and so forth. What an almost jubilant hold on the world of inexplicable phenomena our old friend metaphor has!" I brandish my copy of *Hubble's Universe* before them, displaying almost at random the Cat's Eye Nebula, the Hourglass Nebula, the Egg Nebula, the Tarantula Nebula, the Eagle Nebula (especially, with its trio of three apparent humanoids), and pose my silent query. "Then let me tell you about a craving I once had to write a fiction matching Stephan's Quintet!"

Stephan's Quintet

⚞ Data

A week later I am telling them, but with that costive wince you sometimes feel when you've not managed to do something that was well within your scope. Chagrin. At the time, the idea was most appealing, a chance to exploit one of the biggest areas of the heavens named for just one astronomer (who also happens to have originated an important law of astrophysics). "I was looking at a picture," I tell them, "of Stephan's Quintet, a group of five possibly interacting galaxies originally discovered in 1877. Four of these are receding from us at about six thousand kilometers a second, while the remaining one, NGC (for *New General Catalog*) 7320, the one at lower left in the photograph, is doing only eight hundred kilometers per second. A slow coach. I suppose I had some idea of impersonating or populating these galaxies, keeping four at a distance and bringing the fifth into much closer focus. I must confess that, like other people, I had gotten certain things wrong, believing that the fifth galaxy had a blue shift and was in fact approaching us, and could therefore be personalized in unusual terms — almost a cosmic accost, you might say, and in what Eliot calls Mary's color. Not so, as I later found out. So, if I took on such a structure or design, I had to cope with a slow coach rather than an approach, and all five with a red shift. *In* a red shift, if you get me. I suppose I had the idea of a family in mind."

"Clearly," Mark says, "you weren't going to limit yourself to strictly astronomical data. You were going to make metaphors. I can see the allure of the design, but wonder if it would have had the heft for anything but a short story."

"Just so," I answer. "Maybe that's why I didn't ever do it. I later discovered that 7320 isn't, as formerly thought, connected to the other galaxies by some kind of bridge, which might have been a convenient metaphor to work out in human terms. In fact, it's much closer to us than Stephan thought it was, almost in the cosmic backyard. The other four are a quarter million light-years away. What we now see is that 7320 is merely superimposed on the other four and is an outsider, a photographic artifact, as scientists like to say. Anyway, I didn't do it, though I actually seeded the waters by talking and writing about it, and several people asked when I was going to work on it, and I never was."

"Even though it has musical overtones." Nomi beaming.

"Even though. I could, I suppose, have worked on a similar group called Seyfert's Sextet, but I didn't. I must have become discouraged. I'm talking about this petty flop of mine to demonstrate that you mustn't go off half-cocked, never mind how enthusiastic you feel. The trouble with me then, I suppose, was that I let ideas race away with me. One galaxy was going to be mathematical, another musical, another poetic, a fourth a polar bear quoting Virgil, and the fifth—"

"Yes, the fifth," Vince says, almost caught up in the inert idea. "Tell us."

"A diplomat, maybe. Or an actual space traveler. Or both. Maybe it would have been H. G. Wells coming home to roost from the awkward vacancies of space. I was sure I could fashion the quintet idea into something rich and strange. Stare at the photographs long enough and something's bound to assert itself." I fish one out and pass it around.

"I mean," I add, "if I had wanted to do things properly."

"If we even want to go by properly?" Now, who was that, murmuring behind a hand in front of a face in the crowd? I try once more:

"See how compact the Sextet is, almost a parody of Orion? The other's looser altogether."

Vince again: "Why not do both, a quintet plus a sextet adding up to—"

Who interrupts? "A Tet Offensive!"

"Somebody's right in the groove," I say. "No, I gave up on it, but sometimes in the small hours I linger on the concept, trying to make it flash as other conceits have indeed flashed to my profit. I could have used astronomers, actually. I even thought of Hubble, the American who in just one year at Oxford acquired an English accent. Indeed, it might have worked to have each galaxy speaking with successive degrees of Oxonian suavity, competing."

"Yes," says Michael, "*A Galaxy at Oxford.*"

"If you go on like this," I tell them, "I'll be going back to that old idea and not show for class. OK?"

After a finale that assembles those old favorites Swift, Wells, Bunyan, Browne, and Thoreau, the outsider, we abandon the topic, and I wonder if I'll ever receive from one of them an attempt at my original plan. It is wide open for exploitation on the level of voices, instruments, languages, climates, physiognomy, prose style, and intelligent life, but as it stands at present it is going to go on eluding me. It should have gone into my solitary collection of stories, *The Universe, and Other Fictions,* and it didn't. In those days I was into supplying cosmic objects with human voices ("The Sun in Heat," for example). I tell them this and am surprised to find several have already opened that book and read it closely.

But they have not quite finished with Stephan's Quintet. Tim is already brooding on it, mentioning Claude Simon's use of Orion (Tim really in touch with what's French) and suggesting typographical ways of developing the idea. "Huge print for one," he tells us, "and in different colors."

"Did I ever tell you," I say, "about *Caliban's Filibuster* and Doubleday? The book depicts a flight across the spectrum, so I asked for the tops of the pages to be tinted accordingly—Richard of York Gave Battle in Vain—or having the colors of the pages gradually change. Well, I too gave battle in vain. *Do you think we're made of money,* they said, and that was that."

Dave is remembering something from undergraduate days, when a student handed in a sheaf of papers recalling an orgasm; the sheaf smelled of ammonia, and he'd clearly wiped the paper on the sperm of the moment. The instructor then asked him if he'd considered the problems associated with mass production. There ensues a roar of barbaric glee.

We have gone on too long, with people coming and going for natural relief, stomachs rumbling, eyes glazing, postures declining, wit waning, cordiality cooling. Time to adjourn, and for once we go away as a group to munch on fries and chili around the corner, spurning the Korean Chinese opposite "our" building. We must return to the ransacking of nature, seizing those accidental patterns and paradigms never left alone but humanized almost in haste lest the universe seem too much to handle. Did Lady Murasaki always merit a crater or a double nebula? I wave good night or good evening to whoever said that, only to hear someone out in the hall saying Mia Farrow means "my piglet."

Bells

The hell's bells of the familiar are ringing my ears. Identify and ponder, I hear myself saying so many years ago, the style that suits you best: florid or laconic, austere or lavish. If, after the first few pages, you find yourself resorting to categorical placings (sometimes used by sports writers—the *New Jersey bantamweight*), something's gone wrong and you're wasting details already provided. "Identify and ponder," I more or less say, having said this before, ten or twenty years earlier, "the style that suits you best . . ." On it goes, not so much dutiful as nostalgic, like the day I was lecturing on Shakespeare and heard last year's lecture in my own voice while today my mouth moved not. "Don't be afraid," I say, "to keep on saying *said;* but watch out for elegant variations (*proffered, averred, stated, pronounced, offered, ventured,* et cetera). Don't say just *murmured,* but what kind of murmur, and something like *mock-sneered* especially if you can get at the motives behind it. Beware of hackneyed attitudes to seasons of the year. Nabokov used to hide behind the trees at Cornell and pounce out upon writing students (if he could identify them; he pounced anyway), asking them to name the tree. *Verb. Sap.* In possession of an archetype or myth, remember you can bombard it, graffito it, desecrate it, without damage; it will still shine through. Don't overload on *-ion* endings. Reverse the order now and then: *Into the house he wandered* instead of *He wandered into the house.* Examine your images for latent symbolism; if you want it, then bring to bear the symbolic reputation of your rose, lion, roach, eel, and so on. If not, then undercut the combo with a price, a measurement, an unfamiliar aroma (a rose smelling of camphor and hops). Try to keep opening doors into a character, so as to force the reader to reappraise."

The same happens as before. They write it down with almost creative relish, whereas I, who seem to have had most of these commandments by heart for at least some of my career, can hardly imagine the state of mind that sees them as *discoveries* (Ben Jonson's word for his commonplace book).

"Does it ever," Mark asks, "all come together, not in any

Aristotelian sense, but just as copiously, come together, so that you have, say, a hundred or so interlocked precepts to go by, contending for your attention in any given verbal situation?"

"All the time, Mark. I used to say there are three things worthy of rewriting in every line, which leads to an almost unthinkable amount of work. Go over your prose, I used to say, looking for places in which your energy has waned. I still say it, to myself, thus converting a two-hour stint into a four."

I can see Julia providing an abstract nod, the nod of one recently awakened who finds herself being shoved back into sleep. She agrees, takes a sheepish dekko at the group, and demurely fades.

"Do you," asks Joe, "have all this stuff in mind when you read us? I mean, is it actively up front? If so, I'd expect much more blue pencil."

"I thought for a moment you were going to hit us with *proactive!* Of course not, it's ingrained, but you're right, Joe, in the sense that all kinds of antennae are waiting to nudge. Bells go off, to change the image. I think I see at a glance when a narrator is clearly more interesting than what he/she's narrating. Then I pounce. It's a refreshing situation anyway and should be gratefully exploited. I was thinking about something else. If you want to write about a city, avoid the familiar, and get a little handbook to St. Petersburg, say, preferably an ancient one, as old as you can afford. Do some of it straight, but don't hesitate to specify the odd feeling you get as you walk on the snow. Beneath the snow sit thousands of discarded snowshoes, left there to form a platform geodetic or wickerwork in plan. That's a way to bring St. Petersburg to life. Or make a whole mistake and switch parts of it to the Florida one. Calvino understood this very well. As, to a different extent, did Baudelaire."

Michael is working his way through a yellow tablet, at least half of which he has now rolled under, whereas I would have torn the pages off as I used them.

"Getting it down," he whispers.

"Amanuensis," I say.

"Scribe rather."

"The brief chronicles of abstracted time, or something like it. Y'know."

I used to know. Nowadays I tend to refurbish famous quotes all the time, simply, I suppose, from lack of lectern practice. It comes with age.

"An extraordinary word in an ordinary setting can work wonders," I say, going off at yet another tangent. "Say you have a character who waits for his confidence to *congeal*. That should help, shouldn't it?" They are smiling, wondering how many of *them* I mean.

"Why, none," I say, answering the unposed question. "If, by the way, you repeat a character's name in full, the effect is always one of aloofness; he or she seems so special he/she can't be abbreviated. Canute Hendiadys Poop, for instance, or Bernice Jessamyn Jenrette. It's never any good calling them Can or Hendy, or Neece or Jess, but you might just get away with Poop or Jenrette. Look how the suffixed phrase alters the vibes around the name in the aforementioned 'For Esmé—with Love and Squalor.'"

They all cheer up. Perhaps they feel got at because being instructed rather than chatted with. I don't know. If there was ever a way to take the hard work out of writing, the epic loneliness of deed after deed, the constant bone-bashing butchery that goes on even in the teeth of idyllic fluency, I'd settle for it, at least when teaching, or classing, whatever we call it. Now I go off into a semidream that, responsively, says sometimes suppress one of the senses for an entire page just to see if a reader will notice and, if so, gather from the text something exceptional. You can also depict a person in silhouette, or upside down, in X ray, naked, or as the Beatles' exploding diner — remember? "Remember?" They do. For once my highfalutin world has overlapped with theirs, but I still have no idea who Michael Jackson is, although my mother knew Mick Jagger's mother. Everyone's eclectic. Show a tall person's perspective of self as he/she moves around among people and things, and then a shorter person. Have these people including themselves in their own purview.

Sometimes I stay silent and do not speak, although my mind is racing over familiar hurdles. Other times I speak right up, wishing I hadn't. Rare times, I embark on a sentence that goes nowhere at all, at what seems dizzying speed: "*In the juggernaut lattices of Creation, an agile mind soon learns to—* Finish that sentence by next time, and thank you very much." Now I have said thank you prematurely, and will start again, tweaked by their amusement.

Details

I begin by recommending the West Indian novelist John Hearne and, for good measure, *Helena,* a life of Saint Helena, the woman adjudged to have discovered Christ's cross, by Evelyn Waugh; but I am here to talk about hyperbole, for instance, someone tossing a bead at a wire screen for umpteen years, hoping to wear a hole in it; for instance the widening enumerative span of a story that begins at 11:30 A.M., goes to 11:32 A.M., and so to Tuesday; the third week from now; autumn 1999, say, and so to the eon of Silicon Arrivals. Now I am talking about a harassed student of literature who, obliged to read a two-volume survey over the weekend, compiles a personal anthology from the anthology, selecting one line from each author, thus creating a literary monster of sorts. "Study," I say, "one unusual subject each year: entomology, chocolate making, national flags, hermaphroditism in slugs, rheumatism among sailors. The world is not vague. Most things in it are stupendously precise, which is a safer precept for you than insisting that some snowflakes are identical, or that the more you know where something is the less you know the speed it's traveling at. There are people, I have heard them, who consider specificity a Victorian habit, obsolete since the birth of movies, and write in general terms about everything as if phenomena were simply some prolongation of what philosophers used to call *res extensa*—things stretched out. Please don't. I would hazard the belief, Pollyannaish perhaps, that our own individuality finds its match out there in the world of disparate things. Indeed, by the time the advertisers have finished with us, we may well be less individual than tufts of barley or certain out-of-date trousers presses. Perhaps it is becoming more difficult to keep track of the detail of our lives, not so much of our emotions, which may have minute variants, as of things essential to what we call living successfully—all the required numbers, expenses, procedures to follow—the use of a remote, the burden of the tax code, the apparently simple rules of motoring. Soon, no doubt, we will have nations of clones preoccupied with impersonal details, provoked almost to the point of rage from having to remember, say, that the FAA requires all packages weighing over a pound be weighed at a post office. Or something such. Surely there is a link between the general, superficial mind of the minimalist and the impersonal demands of an intrusive society. Villiers de l'Isle-Adam's cry of *Live? Let our servants do that for us!* isn't far from having to hire a tax accountant, a lawyer, for every move you make." I see I am beginning to let it all hang out, as I well might in a book, but surely not in front of MFAs, who of all people, marooned in a world of incessant entertainment and snooping, deserve a few years' peace.

"That how you feel, Paul?" First Lisa has sprung back to life after a several-week sojourn in the slough of despond. Who am I to know the ins and outs of her private life, her joys and her *crises de cafard*? Perhaps she is going to ask about original sin, on the evidence of world history from the Dark Ages to Buchenwald, and all I would have for her is a Swiftian Irish answer extoling the individual and blaming the mob.

"No, I'm just sounding off. The fine-tuned complexities of modern living are ideal meat for the novelist, but sometimes a real block for the average sensual man/woman. I know people who just can't keep pace with the backroom boys who constantly revise the instructions for computers. The overload incurred for doing simple, no doubt time-wasting things has become a bugbear, hasn't it?" Away from literature and writing we go, only to return as Last Lisa, who may not be bonding with First Lisa after all, both of them alpha women, personifies the ghost of Waugh's Helena (they *do* listen!), who sends off a prayer to the Magi that ends "*Pray always for all the learned, the oblique, the delicate. How do you like that?*" I ask her. She likes it fine, and I tell her it's an odd thing to find in the work of a man whose novels were often short, nasty, and British. "He said an interesting thing about humility as a virtue not propitious to the artist, who in all probability milks his/her own pride, envy, avarice, malice, spite, in order to write, revise, refine, even ruin and renew a work until it comes out right. In doing so, battling against all his loathsome qualities, the artist perhaps contributes more to the world than do the generous and the good, even though he/she may lose his/her own soul in the process. It isn't bad, is it?"

"I prefer that line about the learned, the oblique, the delicate. That's really on the ball. The other notion sounds to me self-serving." Last Lisa.

"Then do read *Helena*," I tell her with my most noble smile, my mind on something that has long bothered me: that people, avid for opinion and bloated with knowledge, spend so much of their lives small-talking about life that they never create anything to be left behind them, and their lives end up a sluice of clichés, street-smarts, and anecdote. I think of Webern's Opus 5, whose acutest, most refined passages therein get whispered at nearly subpianissimo levels. I add to this Proust's contention that a reader tends to give more attention and tenderness to characters in books than to people in real life. I am thinking of Thomas Bernhard's *The Lime Works*, in which the protagonist gets interrupted each time he sits down to compose his masterpiece on hearing, and he concludes there is some kind of conspiracy against him, especially when somebody begins chopping wood. He has been trying to start for twenty years. Two Guinean lads, Yaguine Koita, fifteen, and Fodé Tounkara, fourteen, were found dead in the cargo hold of an airplane in Brussels, in their possession a letter beginning, "Excellencies, gentlemen, and responsible citizens of Europe: It is our great honour and privilege to write to you about our trip and the suffering of the children and youth in Africa. We offer you our most affectionate and respectful salutations. In return, be our support and our help." The letter ended: "And if you find that we have sacrificed our lives, it is because we suffer too much in Africa." Well, in English we have *glower, glance,* and *glimpse,* for all of which French has only *regarder* plus adverbial slipstream. And for all our shining words, *glow* and *glimmer* and *gleam, glitter* and *shuntle* and *glare,* French has only *briller.* How lucky we are, yet how constrained, as this letter to a Chinese party official reveals:

> Respected wise dear teacher leader helmsman pathfinder vanguard pioneer designer bright light torch devil-deflecting mirror dog-beating stick dad mum granddad grandma old ancestor primal ape Supreme Deity Jade Emperor Guanyin Bodhisattva commander-in-chief: You who are busy with ten thousand weighty matters each day, long-suffering one, bad habits die hard and overworked to the point of illness done too often can be habit-forming shouldering heavy responsibilities speeding through the skies powerful and unconstrained

staving off disaster and helping the poor dispelling the evil and ousting the heterodox, you who eliminate rheumatism cold sweats strengthen the Yang and invigorate the spleen the brain who are good for the liver stomach pain relieving and cough repressing, and able to cure constipation.

Surds

"Watching *Blue Velvet* the other night," I explain, "I felt impelled to return to the theme of the enigma, not finding that supposedly enigmatic movie more than faintly puzzling. Somebody called it *The Hardy Boys Go to Hell,* which is amusing, but I think any problems David Lynch has other than with his tumbling, bloated hair have more to do with having to present lengthy transitions within the constraints of a two-hour movie. The sheer speed of the film unrolling deprives you of the chance to look away that a novel, or any other book, provides, and in so doing halts pondering. Lynch doesn't bother to explain what might be mystifying, but he does produce the rough outline of a thriller, which we have met before and have seen explained in several ways. It is quite different with Blanchot's *Thomas the Obscure,* in the course of which you can meditate all you want without getting to the root of things; rather, you float out into the universe after him and his people, as I hope I suggested in that parody of him I read aloud some time ago. The grandstand virtuoso in all this is Beckett, whose *Watt,* whose trilogy—*Molloy, Malone Dies, The Unnameable* (a sobriquet for God)—confronts you with the demented recitative of a mind uselessly talking to itself. That, to me, is real enigma, not some troubling thriller or abstract fable about a doubting Thomas. Am I making this at all clear?"

Dave thinks so, tells me so, but asks about the etymology of *enigma.* "Putting it backward—nearly *imagine.*"

"Just so, Dave. It's a mouthful: *ainissesthai* means to talk in riddles. Now, of your three riddlers, Beckett is the one with afterburners, demonstrating the arrant futility of the mind interrogating itself. Blanchot, for perhaps the same reason as has made him the most invisible French writer, is reticent, couching in abstract language the sense of loss we get when confronted with the inexplicable. As for Lynch, one of the most winning riddles he has is the Dennis Hopper character, who has to resort every now and then to his asthma mask. That's a real puzzle, and it graces him with an almost mineral air."

"Why are we talking riddles?"

"Perhaps because, long ago, the visionary physicist Sir James Jeans said in his *Mysterious Universe,* If you have two thousand radium atoms in a box, all identical, fate will annually knock on the door of just one of them and zap it. Why? When they're all alike? Einstein claimed that God doesn't play games of chance, but that's precisely what Jeans was getting at. Life is always a mystery, as even the Laura Dern character in Lynch's movie observes toward the end. 'Life is strange,' she says, and we have to concede that some force, perhaps the *anagke* force that told even the Greek gods what to do, has something unsolicited and arbitrary in its behavior. Interesting how the Greeks rationalized all kinds of odd developments but handed the casting vote to something as abstract as Hardy's unknowable President of the Immortals. If this is the old version of Camus's absurd, I am not going to argue. Art, ultimately, whether you're pitching suburban domesticity or Faustian metaphysics, has to come to terms with what it cannot fathom. If you're occupied with the mere bizarreries of upscale Westchester living, you won't run headlong that much into the riddles, but if you're writing *King Lear* or *The Unnameable* or *Doktor Faustus* or *The Death of Virgil,* you will, and you won't like it. This is not to push you too far ahead of yourselves; you will soon enough run into the stuff that puts iron into your soul, and then you will perhaps have trouble going on writing as *deinosis,* things at their worst, takes over and slams you with brute fact. Most writers worth their salt, so to speak, manage to assimilate the worst and go on protesting, grumbling, shirking. But you don't have to. Whatever wholesome lens you choose to see life through, you will always eventually glimpse the Gorgon at the other end of your vision. This is not to separate the sheep from the goats, but just to warn you that certain great books can harm you, as I think *Lord Jim* harms you, or *Moby-Dick.* Sorry, I wanted to return to the theme."

"Do you," Christina asks, "think we'd better switch professions already? Teaching or accounting?"

It has happened before; it will happen again. The deepest voice in my mind, a slowly recorded bass, informs them what I am thinking about even as I talk to them, what stuff I am going to save up for myself and the next onslaught of writing. I begin with a witticism: Keir Dullea, gone tomorrow. When two giant galaxies collide, it may take 500 million years for them to slow down enough to merge. They grow tidal tails. *There's* a title. Talent, writes Proust, is a kind of memory, enabling us to recall all the confused music of our days. Commanding the Roman fleet at Misenum, the Elder Pliny, across the gulf from Vesuvius, demanded a boat in which to make a closer inspection of the volcanic cloud, only to receive, somehow, an urgent message from a friend on the other side, "imploring rescue." The Younger Pliny then tells us, "What he had begun in a spirit of inquiry, he completed as a hero. He ordered the quadriremes launched and went on board with the intention of bringing aid to many." Beneath a hail of flaming rubble, he went ashore at Stabiae to rally the population, but right there on the beach died of asphyxiation. He was far from willfully sightseeing. Noël Coward to T. E. Lawrence: "Dear 338171, may I call you 338?" Don Marquis, who helped a cockroach named "archie" to write its autobiography (except the insect couldn't hold down the shift key), once said, "Publishing a book of verse is like dropping a rose petal down the Grand Canyon and waiting for the echo."

Reading a Latin poem by Thomas Traherne, the composer Elliott Carter discovered the following: "I am a flower of air . . . nature's golden joke, its rambling tale, its brief dream, pride of trifles and of grief, sweet and learned vanity, daughter of golden perfidy, and parent of the ready smile." So he wrote Adagio Tenebroso, which tracks the course of a bubble, tootling about above the tumult of human existence. I'll gladly assume the role called *parent of the ready smile.* Only the other day, listening to tuneful Borodin, I witnessed a dancer who, obliged to descend some stairs requiring too much stretch, managed to cover her grimace at the difficulty with a practiced smile, and I admired her for it. Instead of resembling a herniated butterfly, she glided.

She glid. She glode. Revisiting Proust, I find that his phone number was 29205, that he sent his laundry to the Blanchisserie Lavigne, which also did Cocteau's laundry; and that he regularly supplied his mother with detailed accounts of his sleep, peeing, and bowel movements. His father, Adrien, wrote thirty-four books, including manuals on hygiene and fitness, while his brother, Dr. Robert Proust, was the author of *The Surgery of the Female Genitalia* and became so famous for his prostatectomies that people called them Proustatectomies. He once survived being run over by a five-ton coal truck.

An Oxford scholar, whose main other occupation is to compile a *Dictionary of Medieval Latin* (up to L so far), has discovered, he claims, the author of the Anglo-Saxon epic *Beowulf,* in a reversed phrase (lines 887–88 in the poem):

> *He under harne stan,*
> *aethelinges bearn, ana genethde*
> *frecne daede . . .*

which means *he under the gray rock | alone performed the daring deed. Stan Aethel,* or *Aethelstan.* The world is hardly waiting for this news, if news it is, but it pleases me that someone else has loomed out of the historical murk. Aethelstan's deed was to write the poem. Could he have been the same Aethelstan who served as chaplain in the ninth-century court of Alfred the Great? This would date the poem two centuries later than is usual, to the period when Alfred smote the marauding Danes, and so makes *Beowulf* less the barbaric prelude to a less athletic period in English literature, when Alfred translated Boethius's *Consolation of Philosophy.* Indeed, the poem may have been commissioned by Alfred himself for his young grandson, also called Aethelstan. Perhaps *Beowulf* is a companion work to the Boethius, instructing the young king how to defend his homeland, as well as in such subjects as courtly etiquette. This tightening up of the literary fabric, even so long ago, gladdens me, who spent three years laboring at the so-called cruxes in the poem so as to teach MFAs about prose. The poem is remarkably unbelligerent, it's true, and much given to what in music they call *rallentando,* a relenting, or gradual slackening in tempo. No *Iliad* by a long chalk. I do remember certain lines, one of the most effective, if you enjoy that kind of thing, being *Thā cōm Grendel gongan* (Then came Grendel going).

Tell them all this? I think not, but at least Julia seems to have shoved past the NO TRESPASSING signs and taken a full draft of ancient English, to her infinite profit. Surely, after four or five *Alien* movies, we are habituated enough to dragons to stomach a Grendel. In the *Alien* movies, no one speaks of a dragon; it is always the Alien, perhaps to ready us for the last line of *Alien Resurrection,* spoken by Ripley after shocking interludes with the awful miscegenated goofy boy, her son with the long tongue, who ends sucked out of the Betty lander as it comes into view of Earth. "I'm," says Ripley with preternatural calm, "a stranger here myself." In view of her life's turmoil, and her subsequent resurrections, she is in the right, and the line has poignant point.

"May we leave?" It is Last Lisa, puncturing my dream, all of them politely teetering on the edge of their uncomfy chairs. When the dreams begin, about who knows what, I know that a novelist and memoirist is reborn, ready to work. Off they go into the mulled strawberry air of early April.

🖎 Punk Ev

Now it happens again, that urgent look at the adults these youngsters are going to be, except for Michael, who because older shows signs of the man he threatens to be: suave, decisive, with a touch of raffishness, he would have suited well the military of any nation but this, making his mustache a bit more martial, his tone more querulous. As it is, today I decide he seems like a full-blown amaryllis, lurking across the room like a stranger allowed in for his deft manners. Some faces appeal to me on different days, and then I leave them alone, at least in the conjectural abyss of palm-read time. First Lisa reminds me of Sylvia Kristel in a French erotic series starring Emmanuelle: tall, stalking about with a vulnerable air, an innocent receptive face any stranger might misconstrue. Shorter, giving off a glitter that may have come from pain or acute doubt, Last Lisa trembles on the edge of the sardonic, but I know she rarely lets rip with it, at least not in here, the meeting she approached with needless misgiving. It delights me to think of all the gift compressed into these aspirants, who tolerate me and my lettered vagaries as if I am the Elder Pliny, Jack the Ripper, and Buster Keaton rolled into one: not an uncle at all, but what Lear calls a nuncle. I sometimes witness in their perusing avid faces an awareness that this fellow sits at a table almost every day and *does* it, making no excuses (or so they deduce!), no matter how awful he feels, now and then finishing the day's labor with calm, almost chilled beatitude at having once again mastered the furies enough to do his stint at the most taxing, most awesome obligation there is: not art concealing art, in which I don't believe, but art surpassing the art of yesterday—what you did yesterday in triumph, now relegated by something even greener, more adroit. You're finally getting it right! I don't see triumph in *their* faces, but now and then in Mark's a silky bloody-mindedness that augurs well, in Joe's a workmanlike, stubborn resolve never to be satisfied for the next ten years, in Vince's a recognition that humans can excel, top themselves, and so can he. It will come to me in afteryears that, just about unremarked among these injuns, there sat a nonfiction writer called Kathy Long, who not long ago published something of a classic, on clitoridectomy. And we never knew. But the class was always too big, invaded by malcontents from comparative literature, say, or by the French. We became a set, almost a sect, both aesthetic and hard-boiled, I surmise, gabbing about stakes high and sharp. I got to feeling about the class much as I felt, after Matthew Arnold, about the volatile ectoplasm of the novel: "On the breast of that huge Mississippi of falsehood called *History*, a foam-bell more or less is no consequence."

So then, am I partial to them all? It may be. I told them early on I will try to sit inside each person's head, or in each imagination's washroom, but find the shift easier in some than in others. Talk about negative capability or vicarious dalliance! I respond to something Senecan in Joe, the "oldest Roman," with behind him a Catholicism as wily as a green mamba that can do U-turns along itself. In the Lisas, who may avert their faces from being coupled thus, I find the honed blade of determination, an openness to thrill and dismay, a sustained curtsy to the word. Vince, familiar with the poetics of boxing, who drives to class all the way from New Jersey (and back the same day), sees his future in the lissome execution of big sweeping romantic movements apt for bullfighter or soccer star. Of his own emotional makeup, he is sure and may have turned to writing because he sensed he had too much emotion in him to go anywhere else. I wish we had hit on clitoridectomy, as we did on fascism, UFOs (I the only one present who had seen one, I trained in aircraft recognition), farce, and etymology. They knew I had been attacked in the dim recesses of Burrowes Building by a woman with an umbrella, and had dealt with other students wielding razor blades, and B-minuses they wanted changed (I always changed grades downward). None of this bothered them. They'd seen rogue elephants before.

I realize now that, in delving into their faces and mental sets, I was the novelist practicing his paces, as well as the scrutineer of their prose. Certainly they appealed to me as a parade of exotic animals committed to the game of words. There are those who can keep their creative motions private, but not I; I'm sure they saw the little industrious bee within me that crammed the hives and the vales of soul-making; but I have kept them out of my work until now, not so much easy meat as puzzling runes, tempting to know better because I knew a bit; I was the nosey parker held back by the knowing novelist. One day, I told myself, I would site them all at some glorious midsummer picnic near an old railroad line, their studies over, their coffers full, their careers flung upward as so many Technicolor kites held firm by a flesh-cutting string. This, perhaps, is that picnic, in the impressionist manner, or it is a daunting jigsaw puzzle in which Mark, much immersed in the suicides of others, is starting to look fatidic, as he's entitled to. Or Dimitri to become that preposterous sport of punctuated evolution (punk ev), the theory-haunted sheriff, knowing how soft the life of the critic is compared to that of the creative artist *who isn't a mere artisan.* Whether they prosper or not, in this or the afterlife, I vow to link them up with the sources of being and autonomy that Rilke dramatized so chastely. Their Apollo, I told myself, *would* have a bow of burning gold.

Trampling Out
the Vintage

Gape \gaep\ *verb*   mouth ajar, to stare in wonder for a short
moment; or for a long moment, possibly for as long as one is still
alive.   —*Dimitri Anastasopoulos, "The Gaper"*

✄ The High

The thing hardest to talk to them about is the
sense of day-to-day renewal brought about by, almost always,
trying to outdo myself in the fugue of sentences, and then paragraphs and pages. Sheer hard work lies behind this joy, but, par-
adoxically, you don't have to abandon all you managed to do
yesterday; you can build on it, perhaps surpassing it. The feeling
that the wide-open, uncharted domain awaits me each midnight, however lax and poor the day has been, makes the soul
wobble. I draw back from calling this "inspiration" or anything
such; it's just that you might actually be better at it than you
used to be. Some might call it being reborn, and that tempta-

tion increases the older I get: I become an advanced juvenile, confessing that nothing is more stimulating, which at the same time raises my blood pressure and soothes.

Talking about this experience in such tender, halting terms may sound gauche, but who cares? The main thing, in the swoop toward one's latest idea, is to rescue from infancy what remains of unbidden gift. If this is the mystique of writing, of being creative, then I try to pass it on, although the unique core of it remains mercurially private: the thing I do, not so much because I want to as because over the long term, say after seventeen, it was "given" to me to do, my life's portion. It must be religious, even for such a pagan as me.

There is another aspect to this magic, and here I am paraphrasing numerous attempts to tell people, interviewers especially but students too, what the mechanism, the soft machine (to use William Burroughs's excellent phrase), must be. Some people, soldiers in battle or Sigourney Weaver calming herself while alone with the monster in the final capsule ("Star bright," she murmurs), tell themselves soothing things, spout wholesome formulas, to get their souls on an even keel. The voiceovers in Terrence Malick's *The Thin Red Line* do this, reciting as if such stuff had never been thought of before: "The beauty of a serene heart," "The treasury of an undivided love," "The delight of an unspoiled heart," "The mystery of two compatible souls," *piropos* all to some commonplace magic in the matrix of life. The phrases may be less than original, and owe much to sentimental literature, but their role as anodynes is unquestioned, and they go beyond rebuke because they work, restoring faith in a perhaps nonexistent world in which nothing jars, sickens, dies, goes amiss in a million ways. Eden restored.

Well, I think a similar feeling of being smoothed out at the same time as being irradiated occurs in my reborn moments. I am restored to the pastoral, however briefly, to the homogeneous and reassuring, to mother's milk even, and it's then up to me to rally myself in the presence of these calmatives and get on with my work, having been brought up to speed, given back to life. Clearly, in puzzling this out, I am reaching for analogies because the functional equivalent of the sensation is the words themselves, written that day, which is to say that whatever I write—and it need not be in a trance—has symbolic power, coming into being because, for me, the universe has been made briefly whole again and words at their highest power are almost as mysterious as clay, sperm, meat, and spit.

If you tell this kind of stuff to young people, you soon gain a reputation for being off your rocker. No life, they argue, needs anything this mystical to prop it up; I would counter that it's not mystical at all but a form of being supremely revved up. As Plato somewhere says, there is a special virtue in performing an assigned function. Call it efficiency or skill, it reaches heights of some kind and cannot be done without. Diane Ackerman in *Deep Play* talks about this experience, and I am willing to wheel the deep play with words—about which she knows a great deal—under her umbrella. Myself, I would call it enough of the dictionary mobilized in the presence of phenomena, but the label hardly matters, whereas the questing, almost sleepwalking inventiveness does. Deeper I do not go, reluctant to disturb the curd that forms on the teat of paradise, but I honor the impulse as Wordsworth did a daffodil, knowing that without it I would be a mere journeyman.

So this lyrical, gussied-up witness to the ecstatic life (when you have literally been tossed out of yourself into what we now call the zone) endures the hurly-burly of MFA conversation, nobody hanging back because, I suspect, they all have felt something similar. Or feel they should have.

"Every time, a high?" Dimitri wearing his most quizzical smile, but genuinely taken by this alien thought.

"Not when writing book reviews," I josh, "yet sometimes while reading student work!"

They take that in stride, feeling it their due, then press me again. "What if we don't," Nomi asks, "though I'm far from saying I don't. I do."

"Then you become John Galsworthy," I answer. "He must have felt it too, but it came out as three-buttoned suits when it might have been brands like Excalibur, all things bright and beautiful."

"So," Mark muses, "the ecstatic reverie produces an ecstatic or ecstatic-feeling view of things. You write it up because you feel, well, remarkable."

"Kind of. Hard to pin this down. Each to his or her own. There must have been an epiphany even for Galsworthy or Arnold Bennett, yet it comes through as cardboard, worsted, or papier-mâché. Sorry."

But they are moving on, now Vince the romantic leading the charge. He believes me and seems eager to mop up.

"And," Shahid whispers, with an almost chockful lisp, "you like best the work of the people you like best."

⚔ Terrible Swift Sword

The curve or trajectory I have been trying to describe goes past
the delicious instant, the miracle of daily rebirth—both subtly
depicted by that nineteenth-century voluptuary Walter Pater—
into another area altogether, which announces, Here is someone with too much emotion, who feels all things too intensely,
and therefore has to find some other way of expressing how he
feels, perhaps oblique, certainly surreptitious. I freely admit it,
and this must come as a surprise to some, such as a certain rabid
young Scotsman who wrote about me and decided I was a sadist
since I wrote about sadistic things (which nauseated and dumb-
founded me). In my time, serious interpretive critics have
pegged me as a master of liminal thinking (ever on the edge or
brink) or as a ranter, neither of them far from the mark. Small
wonder that, committed to the recurrent marvel of the creative, I piped emotion into a somewhat different channel, away
from ordinary chat anyway. It is not that I came along, as the
song has it, out of nowhere, or out of mohair as a parody of the
song says, out of my genes, but from a military father often too
choked with emotion—too "full," as we say—to speak, and a
wildly responsive pianist of a mother. It figures. The irony, of
course, is that having said as much, I back away from saying
more and, instead, adapt the boundless emotion to what Keats
called the spirit ditties of no tone. I evoke the critic Ernest Milton William Tillyard, whom, one heard, you absolutely had to
know backward to be taken seriously in any interview for ad-
mission to Cambridge. Tillyard specified the driving force of a
literature as conflict between sophisticated surface and "bound-

less primitive feeling." That feeling, perhaps deriving from the snake or horse brain, about which the suicide Arthur Koestler waxed so emphatic. I admit to harboring it and being swept away by it. Heavens, I say, echoing Molière's Monsieur Jourdain, I have been a monster of empathy all these years without knowing it.

I hope the trajectory is clear. These are things I refrain from spelling out in class, for obvious reasons: I feel uneasy, and I prefer writing them out. Some don't. Fine by me. I am not the only pontificator on the loose, nor the only sometimes-reticent one, though my most serious and productive self tends to stay private, writ large in certain works. Certain interviewers in their time have tried to auger their way into what I call my creative center, adducing this or that bit of prose to support their incursion, only to receive a noncommittal nod from the author. They have become auguries instead, predicting their own conclusions.

From the possibly high-flown tone of so much self-examination, I now come to earth with something hard and fast, a terrestrial moral having to do with the synecdoche approach to literature (or any other art). I mean the use of a part for the whole, unveiling Pater but overlooking Ruskin, Carlyle, and Arthur Symons in *their* period, lauding Borges but scanting Cortázar and Adolfo Bioy Casares, installing Wilfred Owen but neglecting Isaac Rosenberg, Edmund Blunden, Edward Thomas, and Siegfried Sassoon. This academe-born, newspaper-inspired tendency to choose in a hurry the representative, almost allegorical personification for an era or even a decade is one of the most pernicious tricks of the trade, a kind of Occam's razor applied to arts, sparing the incurious reader the delights of a literature's length and breadth and converting its spacious variety into what I call homogenes who will stand for the rest, thus easing the literary aspirant's labors. It is long since Eliot held forth on culture in that cantankerous, lopsided study *Notes towards a Definition of Culture,* but he was on song even in its most spastic pages, claiming that culture was "what the people do."

"I am saying," I tell them, "not to believe all you read, and certainly never to believe all you don't read. The air is full these days of semieducated pseudo-Brahmans announcing the disappearance, as achiever and influence, of John Hawkes (fiction's constant rebel), when of course those who saw him as an innovator are still practicing, though not in the bourgeois-suburban-wholesome mode he despised. Many the amateur critics who peddle splinter movements based on their own reading only, or their lunchtime courts-martial. Fewer are those who spot this tendency and warn against it, arguing always for a responsible gaze at the entire corpus of a single author, or of a companionable group."

I am going on, but Christina interrupts, asking, "Why the hell haven't they told us this shit before now? I mean, those who profess——"

"Are supposed to know," Mark interjects.

"Are supposed to inform you of what's going on." She has adopted his rhythm in full cry.

"Not prematurely, though," Mark adds, his thought somehow incomplete, his professor father clearly in mind. "Most of them don't *know.* The best they achieve, unless holding forth about Spenser and Dr. Johnson, is to say somebody is *hot.* It's like people believing in commercials, actually helping some slimy advertiser make a profit."

I hear them out. Their time for discussing how to talk about literature with at least as much awareness as art history graduates talk about *their* discipline is getting smaller. Chances are they won't even remember it as they advance toward a second book. We are whipping the cream of human milk, doing rarefied research like aerodynamicists who spin pilots in a giddy chair. Ten years hence, will they be able to assess Corneille's hero cult against Molière's bourgeoisie, or Durrell's sumptuousness against Pater's? All one can hope for is that, at an earlier age, some seed got planted that will fructify, most of all when they take up arms against a sea of infidels. A liberal education is hardly likely to set you free, but it may warm up your chains.

"If I may," Christina is continuing, "what is the connection for you between your magical rebirth at the worktable and this tendency to distort reputations? Is there a connection at all?"

"You may end up," I answer, "the only critic or thinker who gets you to rights, and so you take your stand on what you know about yourself, not on what others have said. They can never strip you of the glory from day to day, which has little to do with them. I'm giving you an optimist's treasure trove."

"Rather than an *Optimist's Daughter*!" Just so. Who was that, chipping in? Shahid, coming to life? Too short for him, who thinks in longer periods. Then who?

I have started something I wish I hadn't. To do this, you have to be in the thick of things, publishing and arguing, not in the forecourt of letters. Otherwise you have to be budding critic, sweeping the distance with an impartial glass. This is to engage them in prematurity, but, oddly enough, they care more about gathering a reputation before they have written anything. It's as if the chivalry came first, the manners and mores, the set of the writer's jib, because most of what people hear is founded on gossip anyway, especially when some pundit says the novel is kaput (echo of the sixties' dead or dying novel), replaced by a formulaic street-smart TV police soap called *Law & Order.* An ostensibly serious article making this very point appeared at the end of the last century. "Write your stuff," I tell them, "don't listen in! Figure out what that pop philosopher called *your bliss* and stay with it, come what may. Otherwise you'll not respect yourself in the morning. When a publisher tells you, as I have been told, he'll give you more money if you'll agree to class your novel as nonfiction, look away toward Proust's tower of Roubaix."

"Who was that?"

"He of the bony shoulder blades," I say, shaking my head at his vision of the Swan of Tuonela's undulating line swum between the zones of life and death, tempted both ways. I may not know the differences between fiction and its alleged opposite, but I do know that words are fictional.

Paper Fugue

Jim, as we obligingly call Dimitri, wishing he would change his surname (Anastasopoulos) instead, hails from a school quite contrary to the one that spawns seafaring yarns for overgrown schoolboys, scanting both Melville and Conrad in the act. He excels at parallel writing, which is to say narrative that exploits the etymology of narrative words. Time and again, instead of getting on with his tale, he drifts sideways into word origins, frustrating all who search for plot, both page turners and speed readers. This is only fair in that far too many fiction writers write the same story, as unaware of their rivals as a dog is unaware of Descartes's adventures in the hot cupboard. Dimitri fascinates because he knows enough to get away with it, amassing not so much action as the verbal history of his plot, which he celebrates by recalling its other plots (Minsk while roaming Helsinki) and transforming it often into sexual terms. Never wasted on him, my early advice to grab an out-of-date guidebook to St. Petersburg, and exploit it contrary to fact, looms in front of him, allowing all visible cities to become in part invisible. He alters everything as he goes, making it more real than the tourist can because it's related to some intellectual mainstream: the alien's, the word expert's, the erotic worrier. Abandon all preconceptions, you who enter here, recovering if you can from the opening sentence (if indeed that's what it is in "The Gaper"). I begin exemplifying.

"A hostile reader or a rival etymologist may go after him for not offering the reader enough clues, whereas of course he offers so many that merely have to be digested at something beyond normal speed. It will be possible to piece the story together from Sibelius Park, toilet flush into the Baltic, ice-tray vodka, Minsk masturbation, methods of snaring women, machismic underwear, the Hotel Marksi, Suomi brew, the Café Manta, loamy massages, the twenty-markka fee. And the vampirettes. You get what he calls 'a paper fugue' in one of the most miserable countries known. In Finland they are always waiting for someone to arrive and cheer them up. This is the riff he selects, though subduing it beneath a froth of word history, and not even a journey through Joyce will ready you for the outcome. The story, so-called, teaches you how to read it as it advances, en passant giving you a hint as to how the mind of a normal man cavorts while writing about such a morose world. What is he doing here in the first place? What on earth was he doing in Minsk? The amazing thing, of course, is how closely he comes to delineating the Finland that is, in other words, Helsinki. Does this fair city not repose on the myth that the Finns, not the Swedes, are the sexual athletes of Europe?"

I ask them, who have been stunned a little by Dimitri's constant oblique parallels, but they don't give a hoot about that. They worry much more about his juicy introversion, the constant threat that he can always make more of a phenomenon than it deserves. This verbal fecundity distracts them from that old canard the story line and promises Dimitri a difficult publishing career because he can always think of something new to say before shifting from one event to the next, a paradigm for which is his almost spastic opening paragraph. I read it aloud, just to get the flavor across.

> "Up already, flying over the august fishback of a ghost cloud, above the portrait of a city still swooning within the cerebral gutters of at least one *babushka*—populated with flourishing swans and young tongue-cluck girls, bird droppings littering the space above letters in their names (the symbol above the *å* for instance)—a city

animated with trams gorged on the emissions of red-faced drunks from nearby Porvoo, and a cobblestone walk leading to an intact World War II submarine (did the Finnish really fight?), a once-sequestered typer from Minsk looked upon the whole of this spume, its streets, or her streets if he'd remembered her epithet "the daughter of the Baltic," flushed into a chowder of a harbor into which the city's wastes extended. Who would have thought: Helsinki?

"You see, he has already considered, and disdained, using this as the second or blah-blah paragraph, opting for impromptu complexity over the straightforward and rectilinear. He wanted to begin 'Up already,' which drives the reader in several directions, all pleasurable, capping the phrase with *fishback, cerebral, babushka, the symbol above å,* and so forth, offering us almost too much, at least until we recognize his way is *always* to offer us too much, because this is how his rubberneck mind works, whether his makeup is Greek-speaking Russian or Finn or not. In a sense, in his first paragraph, he already offers us a vignette that other writers would have presented with delayed action over several pages. Dimitri hurries us in, primes us for more, and, working a priori, gives us an epitome without spelling out all the details, like Herodotus in a hurry."

"Isn't it turgid, then?" Our first response.

"Read slowly," says Mark, "it isn't turgid. I think that's the wrong word. More likely a vodka ice cube on which to suck yourself to death while the pseudo-story goes on. I think this is utterly typical of Dimitri's work. What else would you expect of work with a Rocketsch in it? None of it bothers me. It's not so much that I resent the way it's written as that I'm glad I didn't have to write it. It seems to demand a great deal of the writer."

The vision of Mark as a lazybones, with his six sure-handed novels, amazes me, but the fine air of that mountaintop must do odd things to him. I ask some others, none of them Finns, all daunted a little by Dimitri's centrifugal references. "What about the flying?"

"Actually," says quiescent Julia, "it reminds me a bit of Virginia Woolf's essay 'Flying Over London.' Clearly, Helsinki's a curio, an old curiosity shop you might not want to visit. I'm just wondering, though, if, after you've launched out into a cameo, a vignette, you can then spell out in the usual way the phenomena in what seems the right order. I mean, OK to be pithy, concise, but doesn't being so commit you to a technique to be used throughout? Myself, I might have spelled things out straightforwardly by putting para one first, then followed up with the synthesis, the captious synthesis, of the first para. I'd have the sense of having gotten away with more."

I wonder how Dimitri, having committed himself to the other way, likes this, but he has assumed a Finnish expression for the rest of the afternoon. We are not going to get an argument from him, at least not one in which he's the victim.

"Wasn't *grok* once a fashionable word, in the sixties? Sort of Krushchevy? No, long before that. Between Molotov and some other guy? Didn't *grok* mean to dig or like?"

Less interest they could not show. "Screw the sixties, it was before we were born," nobody says. I withdraw and try with Helsinki again. "What do you make of this? Here's a writer in-

tent on crafting perfect sentences, but he's held back much of
the time because so many things occur to him that they mar
the shape of his sentences. Trying to get so much in, he sometimes gets untidy, sworn to constant parentheses and as many
dashes as the essayist Osbert Sitwell. I detect an urge to force the
story onward, but swerving always to the side to take in the latest oxbow lake, if you'll forgive the image."

A few do, but with nods only. "I think he's invented a new
word, *typer,* for all of us." Christina comes to life with her best
empirical grin, "but isn't it obsolete already? And doesn't that
tell you something about the nature of our narrator, a bit out-
of-touch and out-of-date? After all, he's not using a stylus, but
he's no hypermodernist, either." This must be a private joke
with Dimitri, not ours to share, but Michael leaps in: "He's the
guy who brings it all to life as if recovering the dead. Doesn't
Helsinki appear quite often on *60 Minutes,* lord knows why,
dances and such, without their hearts ever being in it? There's a
good story waiting to be written about the saddest city in the
world. I don't think this is it; it's about Dimitri's imagination,
really—and what a lovely one to have—but it's constantly addressing itself when it need not. Am I making sense? This isn't
Helsinki, it's Dimitrisinki, almost an *apologia pro imaginatio sua.*"
Nomi thrills to hear someone addressing her in her native
tongue.

Whatever problems Michael has with Finns, Dimitri has
worse with the American pragmatic way, composing cerebral
fiction in a land that, far more than Missouri the Show-Me State,
requires its denizens know what to do next, never to be at a loss
in the domain of action, like certain sergeants in the military

who show the officers how. Something mellowly introverted hinders him and makes his work seem hard to follow because, to put it bluntly, he tends to get lost in his prose and the meditations that support it. If this is not fatal in America, it's wounding, and it has done damage to such as Melville, Faulkner, and Henry James, but has been kinder to the Fitzgeralds and the Steinbecks than they deserve. Where exactly this prejudice against thought comes from—perhaps the burst of initiative that founded the republic, the decisive acts of defiance that sustained it—is hard to gauge, but one encounters it not only in the cult of knowing what to do next, but also in the no-nonsense prose of those who know the country is mostly behind them and not behind those who find the texture of life engrossing, the thoughts and perceptions occasioned by what gets done. Check through the schools of prose writing and find the no-nonsense criterion solidly established, the list of self-indulgent malefactors clearly posted, behaving as if they were French or Spanish. The English too have their version of this, only too readily dismissing Woolf and company as pansy writers besotted with surfaces and subconversation, as Sarraute calls it. I suppose the view never dies that fiction should be matter-of-fact and straightforward because anything further demands thought, and this is something for which the high schools have trained almost nobody.

So there is an almost purblind obtuseness in readers' responses, akin to finding literary narrative immoral and fancy, not to be taken as it's intended. If there is a backlash against fiction, more in the closing years of the last century than in the sixties, say, it has to do with what will please advertisers and movie producers. In this world of the up-front obvious, it seems almost cowardly not to know what to do next, or to have your characters do, apart from savoring the Zeitgeist or the weather, the ways people have of shaking hands, say, or their response to a witty turn of phrase. All this gangs up on the Dimitris, the Julias, the First Lisas, them at least, as they go their besieged way into literature and out of it, welcomed by the discerning few, evicted by the unwashed many. They are unlikely ever to refrain from their given cast of mind—meditative, allusive, conjectural—so there is virtually no way of bringing them to book. Intransigent they remain, convinced that one of the charms of the brain is its capacity to taste and applaud the flow of life, the impress of both gross and refined behavior on the cells. It is no use arguing with them in some battle of the books inherited from Swift. From among their ranks will come the stylists, who believe in style as a unique thing more worth developing than mere action, though it is this last that occupies most of the fiction writers alive today, who, having been taught their lesson in the Gradgrind for-profit school, commit themselves to it with sentimental righteousness.

I am therefore loath to hammer away at Dimitri for doing what I admire, and practice myself, even though I sometimes hurl my characters into action, for the sake of contrast. And when something arrives for comment or support—by Ingeborg Bachman, Roa Bastos, Frame, Magris, Morrow, John Vernon, I just about know I'm getting something ample, suave, mandarin, eloquent, patient, poised, articulate—to pick words hardly ever used on the Rialto except to express abuse. Why, you even find business managers reviewing works of delicate art, their MBAs hot in their pocket, their blood up to see justice done to Hemingway, himself the unnoticed mauve aesthete of the prose corrida. Ignoramuses abound, churning out their uniform banalities as if typing were literature, and the Dimitris go forward to a certain future, already persuaded enough about the delicacy and subtlety of their calling not to abandon it, never mind who says what. I laud them, as Matthew Arnold said, not so much to change anything as to keep alive a needed attitude.

Christina's Goth

They say that my friend, that extraordinary swank and peddler of
keys, old Vicky Tin, wasn't born with his hump. It certainly doesn't
appear in the few remaining pictures of his youth, the ones his
mother didn't burn in one drunk or another.

> —*Christina Milletti,* Vic Tin: Locksmith
> Secret-Keeper Extraordinaire

⬚ Vic Tin

Christina is one of those writers with dense
awareness of the world around them, which hems in the people
and provides solid ballast for musing, spectatorial sentences.
This is always a plus, though it tends to mean that her characters have to display uncommon energy or presence in order to
compete with context. In other words, as I see it, she cannot
afford to deal in what philosophers used to call universals—
saying "dog kennel" for all dog kennels, and indeed accumulating such sentences as "The taller of the two took out his
penknife, gift from his mother, opened it, and looked at the
horizon where rain was gathering." Impatient or shallow readers demand no more; after all, they are accustomed to being

supplied with landscape even by the movies, which fill in the blanks of all universals as best they can. At this level of incuriosity, what the English call railway reading, the reader can be supplied and does not need to remember what he/she will forget anyway, supplied with filler by what Auden, speaking of emotions, called "an efficient band." She does not do this, careful always to equip a reader with enough mise-en-scène to match the reading's length. And to do this on a regular basis, of course, helps install in the writer's imagination a keen, almost tender awareness of "all things bright and beautiful," as well as of things less wholesome. So there's a distinct advantage to starting with a developed response to the world akin to Woolf's kneel-on-the-grass and be grateful.

That fixed in my mind, I can get to Christina's *Vic Tin* and his hump that's a visitation from Uncle Fred. "Notice in the opening paragraph," I say, "that the shtick about the hump almost figures as the hump itself, a hump in the throat if you like, the hump growing with the prose. We then read *some say Vic's hump was a visitation from Fred* and quickly gather what level of magic we're functioning at. If this be magical realism, it has mild teeth, amenable to the very idea that a hump is almost as good as a brother. To my mind, that makes for an inventive, yet unspectacular opening to be followed up, as indeed it is, especially with such outlandish characters as Herr Frank with his— what would you call it?—*plattdeutsch* accent and dimissory view of American speech. I'm not sure why, but these friendly caricatures remind me of Mussorgksy's *Pictures at an Exhibition,* perhaps too of Respighi's most bombastic glimpses. We speedily gain an idea of Vic, for whom work is a game. This makes the world wide open, exposing us to other kinds of work-obsessed creatures. A bellhop by trade, Vic also evokes for me the be-whiskered, puffing, self-important flunky commissionaire in F. W. Murnau's movie *The Last Laugh,* in which the protagonist ends up swabbing out underground toilets.

"The big thing about Vic is that he has no formal title and so might be construed as an odd-job man, a jack-of-all-trades and deformed to boot. Yet he is more than a repairman; he's a lov-ing observer, a Proust of the drainpipe, who adores to watch things change and grow, with his girth bending him forward, the hump backward, so that he seems rooted to the spot, a cranky old tree, an ageless automaton. Add to this vision the management's idea that Vicky Tin is implicit, the caretaker writ large. Everything implies him, demands him, could not exist without him. We have heard of people whose work owns them. Well, he is one of them, but he is also that elegant entity the reminder, the presence that reminds us all of what we live among, in this case the hotel's body. It was Ortega who said women invented work, men invented love. Vic has just perhaps been invented by the hotel itself to keep the armature in run-ning order. We have met such people, unable to imagine them doing anything else, and have taken their grandeur as some-thing approaching sainthood: certain warrant officers (gunnies, say), certain ticket agents, certain blind sellers of bootlaces.

"It is to Christina's enormous credit that she has been able to construct such a personage, crafting him gently this side of the zoo line, say, insinuating into the presentation other not necessarily intertwined factors—the hump, the word *implicit,* other kinds of workers, Herr Frank's words *Hund* and *Zopf,* other bellhops, and the bulging repertoire of his reputation, growing out of the title (Locksmith, Secret-Keeper Extraordinaire) in which the last word corks the bottle with an indefinable plug. Here cometh everybody, as Joyce says. The first few pages of Christina's piece do some exemplary work, ringing the changes with polite zest and persuading us that we are on the doorstep of a novel. I cannot think we're not, with a presentation so searched, so trenchant, so—I'm sorry—polyfilamental. There's enough up front to energize a novel for several chapters, even if not psychologically searching.

"Then we discover Vic in his role as caretaker of the Maftis, whose locked-up daughter evokes many a romantic heroine of noirest hue. When we are introduced to the idea of two types of seeing, I at once think of the Chaucer who, Matthew Arnold claimed, lacked high seriousness. I mean Chaucer was a terrific observer and listener, but also, in a minor, derivative way, an intruding spirit. O that he had intruded more! On the level of imagination, I don't see why the young Mafti should not develop into a 337-year-old opera star as in Janáček's opera *The Makropoulos Affair.* The entire idea of humpy Vic going up and down stairs to tend to the ménage Mafti while she, pent up, recalls performances from back in the seventeenth century, stirs my mind. Perhaps she is to become a time traveler. Yes, Michael?"

"May I? Something occurred."

"Let it, by all means."

"Don't we notice a difference in tone, a development that announces increasing confidence as well as a yearning to speculate more and more, moving sideways and to and fro? To my mind, this is when a novel begins to cook, when those liberties to be taken get taken. Isn't there a kind of logic that says, if you have a factotum with a hump, an omnicompetent locksmith and all the perks appertaining thereto, isn't it almost *logical* (not to mention pertinent) to have a young-old woman who's been locked up for forty years? Seems to me, folks, the novel begins to take off when we realize we have two larger-than-life, maybe larger-than-death, presences, to use Paul's word. As the prose tells us, the daughter brings mystery into the bellhop's life and into ours, too. He hasn't seen her face since youth. The mention of the pinhole reminds me of Trevor Howard in *White Mischief,* his last movie, when, after inviting Greta Scacchi to board with him in the wilds of Kenya, he lets her get settled in the tub and then hies to the secret pinhole in a cabinet and gets an eyeful. *An unreliable view,* we're told. The space no bigger than his body. The vision of a gradually aging female is the gift that keeps on giving. She has nowhere else to go."

These things having been taken care of, as Caesar used to write, I move on to a less charitable view of "Abbastanza," the next installment, short at that. "Christina, if this is intended to take us into the psychology and long incarceration of the daughter, I think it's far too short. Not that I find anything in it as it stands that doesn't work. It's just that you ought to go back and lengthen it. Unless you mean to fix on Vic throughout, this won't quite work as even the first delve into processes. She's decided to appear, she's had a dream of the outside world, figs and toast will tempt her for breakfast. Lovely and all, but it in no way balances the rest, what has preceded and what's to come. Can we put it this way that you will develop it as she needs? Maybe I'm on the wrong track and you intend something else, but I can't imagine this two-page interruption ballasts any portrait of her needs. Papa has gone and she vows to come out of her self-imposed closet, but at the last minute she slams the door and heads back into the apartment, leaving her hair like *a web in the door,* as you exquisitely depict it. It's just a sketch, isn't it?"

"Are you coming back to *me?*" Michael puts this plaintively, and I salute him. "Whenever I come back to you, Michael, it will have to be copious. Excellent points all. Let me just finish first. There follows the section entitled 'Herr Frank,' stylistically a severe but welcome contrast, though you seem more interested in him and his Dickensian sound effects than in your female prisoner of belated name. I just wonder if your intervening section, so short, would look different if much longer, and how this section itself would appear, especially with the Mafti father a stuffed corpse. Even Mussolini puts in an appearance here, and the Romans, followed by Signor Battini's Consulate memo printed in a tall, narrow, angular column, just like one of the ruins knocked about a bit, confirming that the daughter's name was Abbastanza, to my mind a brilliant encapsulation piece, like a roving segment from a completely outside point of view, filling us in, and in, and in. We end in a world of typewriter keys and automotive pistons, both of which they manufacture back in Italy. Dated 1949. Clearly you had a choice here between the abruptness and curtness of the short story and the fat divagations of the novel proper, and you made it. I just want to urge you to go back to this material and plumb it as it deserves to be plumbed. At the moment it has a Tennysonian feel to it, or an echo of Chaucer's 'The Knight's Tale,' with lovers locked in towers, but I look forward to the extended version in which the

Italian and American layers would have full play, and Abba-stanza's complex your full attention. She, it seems to me, is the heart of the whole thing, but right now she's undivulged like the toy that rattles around in an unpulled Christmas cracker. The enigmas of the work fascinate me too, but the explanations might blow my mind completely. Now, back to Michael."

"I'm not so sure all that gabble's worthy," he says. "I could have honed it before inflicting it on you all. It's just that I felt myself vibrating with the piece, especially with the access in the manner of delivery. She does the police in different voices. You could make a case for the short story surrounding the mysteri-ous daughter like an octopus, and you'd classify it—not *you,* but *one*—as enigma variation. I too would gain more from Ab-bastanza's novel, in which Christina might shuffle all manner of things: the primitive and the technological, the first-person phonetic and the distant, omnipotent third person, et cetera. A good chunk of raw material to have fun with, but none of it as good as the opening blast. I especially like the suggestion that the father was a spy, which in Texas, as Paul says, they call a *spa.* I detect a flurry of possible plots all interacting, with raw coin-cidence taking over now and then. I liked it, Christina, and ad-mire the maturity of its structure."

It is the cheerfulness in Michael's demeanor that warms his severity. He sometimes speaks like an authority who has been discredited, for unknown reasons, and I deduce this is how he used to hold forth at the university TV station. "Michael," I tell him, "you're doing it again. You're on the ball today, so you don't mind giving us an earful. Perhaps the book isn't experi-mental enough. There, I've called it a book."

Now the chiming of opinions starts, picks up.

"Mind-provoking and pithy stuff."

"I wanted more, a whole raft of craft."

"They're absorbing characters, don't waste them, don't throw them away, live with them a year!"

"A loss of energy in the middle, as if that herculean climb or trek were too much for you at that time of the writing. Go back and beef it up, yes."

"It's so *considered,* so firm, that it makes the intervening Abbastanza bit a bit like a wafer of balsa wood."

"Myself," I say to no one in particular, "it's what Cortázar would call a model kit—something to be assembled from pieces that rattle around in a box. As we saw not long ago."

"Plus the addition of glue that smells like nail polish?" Michael is not to be outdone. Having launched twice, he flies onward, ever higher. We are sharing a boyhood idyll of the toy that comes in a box and ends up, sleek and torpedo-like on the piano, still faintly garbed in peardrop aroma.

At last Christina stirs, only to part her lips without speaking, as if receiving the host at Communion, a ritual I the pagan have heard about. She is wise to keep her own counsel, but she has at least nodded a lot, almost as if nodding were a new form of erudite discussion. You can almost hear her wheels whirring as she takes it all in. It is unique to watch someone newly creative settling our comments and obiter dicta into nests built into the terminal moraine of Mussolini, whose role in all this remains inscrutable, which is part of the fun.

"These are portraits," I say, "imaginary portraits, hung in the gallery of Italy. There's actually an entire book about the

Italian novel in America, I mean the novels of Italians who live in America. Not bad either." I am trying to recall the author's name when Mark sighs, pounds his hefty fist on the table, and delivers himself of a Gulliver nod. "It's as if she's stationed lily pads all over the place, some historical and some not, and the reader is a stilt bird stepping from one to the next, and it sinks a little under even that tiny pressure." He likes it.

Searching, I am thinking. That piece about the locked-up daughter should be more searching. That was the word my mother used when describing the effect of brussels sprouts on her innards. "Too *searching* for me," she'd jest, "so I am happy to cook them for others, but not for me. Too ..." Ah yes, beware the searching sprout. It is time to dabble with the literary fate of someone else, even as the pressures of ending the semester grow and the heap of stuff in our mailboxes gets bigger. We are coming to *an* end, if not *the*.

Joe's Indent

I first met John Nibbs near the groundhog hole in the cemetery. He was jogging frantically around a headstone, slapping his knees with his palms and puffing grief with his chin. Never had I witnessed such discipline coupled with misery. —*Joe Schall, "A Different Letter"*

✑ His Nibbs

I first met Joe when he was an undergraduate in a not very enterprising group of would-be fiction writers, some of whom showed no promise in English at all. I think that was my last go with undergrads, after which I declined to mess with them further—I was teaching *grammar,* fun indeed, but nothing creative because they were simply not ready for it. Joe was a puzzled-looking, serious, muscular fellow who seemed to linger on my every word, appraising and putting it into his electron microscope. I soon found that talking to him about fiction was a bit like living in Lord Salisbury's country home, where they threw books up at the ceiling to quell electrical fires that burst out along the newly installed cables. In private, Joe told me about his obsession, as I remember it, with a certain Rob Funk, a bizarre oddball from his childhood who kept getting stuck in awkward situations with incongruous things (I improvise: a baby's rattle, a live rattler, becoming a baby's rattle, unthreatening again). In this way, from an early age, Joe had developed his liking for outlandish characters, executed in blunt, farcical terms, not that he knew then that he would win a prize for stories, a national one too; he was only doodling with evolution, a horror of dentists, and a bestiary cooked up from some expressionist dimension within. It was fascinating to see his stories get bolder, more savage in an understated way, as if he had decided that, so long as he remained calm about life's rough-and-tumble, he could make heavy inroads on its idiocy. How pleasant to discover him, a year later, placing stories with this or that magazine, who not long ago was doing prentice work in a class of putrid wanna-bes. Up by his bootstraps came Joe, conjurer of travesty, a divagator who got off the beaten track from the first sentence on.

He didn't rush, to please or to goad himself. So far as I recall, he kept at the same speed all the time as if addressing himself to something that would occupy half a century anyway. He appeared not to fret or to delve too deep, but he carved stern caricatures on the surface, sure of himself whatever anyone else was doing, and modeled on—I had no idea whom, but I knew he was a devout Catholic with that special fatalistic cordiality of Catholic satirists. He wrote to please himself, in the first place anyway, and he somehow seemed to be relating all his personages to the freakish stunts of Rob Funk, childhood behavioral obscurantist who had won him over like a Martin Short from

Mars. You learned this from Joe: to stay still and quiet while noting every detail of the human zoo. I found him a long way from what mattered to me, but I enjoyed his élan vital and his faultless addiction to ridicule.

Today we are looking at "A Different Letter," a story in which Joe has managed to incorporate parts of his early and current life, making himself his own raw material, distanced of course and given a redshift to help it on its way to Betelgeuse. He also manages to milk the kind of prose we used to get, and weep over, in that undergraduate English course where he began, now made over into what we amusedly call a work of art. The amazing thing he pulls off is the use of banal stuff from banal lives, cemented together in a rickety structure until it makes you shudder for the human condition, as in the hygienic triangle within Marjorie Heffelfinger's shambles of a kitchen. The true killer to her mess is her Aliquippa hair, which never moves. I read aloud, from a typescript on this occasion, so as not to make the rest uneasy.

> "It was not like a bristly, mesh, agrarian, convoluted, iron-gray, infested fortress because no words could describe it. It just sat there. . . .

"Notice how he writes, *Normally, when I am flabbergasted* . . . to give an especial edge to our disbelief, the key to the whole being that nobody has ever said quite that before, so we get originality on top of his report. It has been observed before, but only by flabbergasted folk."

"Blame John Nibbs." Mark.

"He's cruel, what with her kitchen mess, knee-high, all those one-way streets in Huntingdon, John Nibbs's commitment, and *the milk filling his right shoe.* If all that can happen, aren't we getting close to sadism?" Sally, perhaps missing the way the story absentmindedly assembles itself from a thousand maltreated particulars, none of which adds up to any kind of fulfilled life. "He soon gets into the idiocy of those who think the moon a dead star, trying to reach, or have somebody reach, what he calls the zero of unthought, aspiring rather boldly, after having read Beckett, to think his mind to a halt. To make my thoughts stop, he says. *A Real Story* by John Nibbs, September 28, 1992, actually entitled *The Process,* has profound beginnings, in a man obsessed about finishing a thought without dying—*without dying, remember,* as the urgent footnote cautions us. This metaphysical craving, coupled to Marjorie's mess, covers a wide span of human experience with an adroit, cock-a-hoop touch, as is usual with Joe. In theory, if you make up a story about nothing, then it will have nothing in it, and therefore will give you no trouble when you want to end it. Poor Nibbs, His or otherwise. The phrase His Nibbs—potent as an alkaline battery, means someone prey to self-importance. As I was saying, the perdurable nothing won't let you get away with anything. The minute you try to think of nothing, something intervenes."

I look at the glee in Joe's boyish face, noting the tease in the grave stare, knowing he has outwitted us before we even speak. "The shocking irony about this story is that everything that's in it proves his point: the inability to think the mind to a halt, the way every discernible something always leads to something else, the ever-elusive tabula rasa, which contains the thought of its own emptiness and can therefore be considered a pouch. Off goes John Nibbs in quest of more unstories, akin to Joe's dentist who loads his apartment with thought-provoking dental paraphernalia (a word Joe dotes on), the woman who modifies her menopause by changing her diet (or so she thinks), the English major, one of my favorites, pioneering serious pseudoscientific articles—a new genre, fit for Swiftian fantastic projectors. Sometimes Joe reminds me of another outlandish projector, the Pole Witold Gombrowicz, himself once lost in the sleepwalking immobility of Argentina. He took a boat and never got back for more than a quarter of a century. It was nature that smothered him; wherever he looked, he found it, choking and humiliating. In the same kind of matter-of-fact prose, Gombrowicz tempts us to believe in the paradise at which we dare not look. Joe, too, except that Joe has America to contend with, and all its *stuff.* Surely, if anything, the American dream is a dream of *stuff,* not of abstract ideas or nothingness, but available, buyable trash. Closer to our human sedition, rather than condition, Joe gives one character asthma, much as he might adduce another's sinusitis, epilepsy, stammer. It's not so much that we all have something, as folk wisdom insists, but that it has us, from birth or even earlier. Behind Joe's ironic curlicues lie our genes, the givens, the *données,* of involuntary experience. No wonder we hunger for some tabula rasa, a clean-shaved mental chin (for men at least)."

"Something Kafka-like." Vince for once, no doubt pondering the geography of that long return drive, a pattern he is as much locked into as into peristalsis.

"Yet," insists Christina, "he makes it all so optional, in so genial a manner, if you read all his stories, an affable prankster comes out, despairing maybe, paranoid by prescription and definition, but one of us, the vox humana amid the pax humana."

"Or the pox humana," Joe says, illicitly chiming in.

"I think he owes something to Boris Vian, whose *Empire-Builders* always haunts me with its Michelin man, whom they all, those on stage, beat into submission: the *Schmurz.*" I ask him. No, he has not seen the *Schmurz,* but he would like to. The question is how? "Go to New York," I say. "Then, *I* don't know. You'd have to search."

"Or read him," Joe says, and the ball is back in the disjointed tennis court of his smashes and lobs, all lines triple and awry.

Something has happened here that has happened before, as when almost anything in print, or rumored to be so, has appeared on the table, in the cardboard box in the mail room. The discussion shades over from gentle kibbitzing of a work in progress (maybe) to a discussion of literature, as if now and then the class installs one of its own in the canon. Even if only for practice, this has to be good because it enforces out of the unspoken alliance standards that aren't merely sympathetic. The class makes its own moves, of course, already familiar with my so-called doctrine of criticism: the genial, and the non-. The second kind *doesn't* judge by what the author's trying to do, it sets her/him alongside Faulkner and Kipling, Beckett and Colette, and asks if the thing under the microscope is any good, clearly something that must be taken seriously, even if offensive. A harsh standard? Certainly, when you test Jane Austen against Faulkner (unless they both deal with villages!), more so

when you try Aubrey Beardsley against Céline. We don't usually practice type 2, except in literature courses, but it's good
when, sometimes, the Medusa raises its ugly head and sets us
off comparing, and exposing a remediable weakness, say, a refusal to swing with the pliability of the imagination or to persist
in a current of action over an entire chapter. Most of these
people have published, so their feet are already wet, undried.

I look at Joe, faintly blurred by his own fame, and wonder
if he knows how close he comes to Danny Kaye and Buster
Keaton, whose personages keep running into strange predica-
ments with humdrum things, appliances or ladders, clearly displaying bald Gibraltars in their personalities: proxies for misfit
authors combing through their own nightmares.

An eager, unrepentant face is looking at me as I sink exhausted into the almost surgical chair I occupy. She is apologizing
for sitting in, snooping, eavesdropping, and explains that she is
writing a family history that, if she is lucky, Bantam will publish.
This is Joann Leonard, a faculty wife with a courteous demeanor,
passionate about the sentence, she says. Or passionate about
being passionate about it. "May I sit in?" Here comes another.

"Toughest, most rewarding of all the conundrums," I tell
her, ready for sleep. "Crack *that,* and you're home well, if not
free, at least in platinum chains. Sure, go ahead. Maybe you'd
better scrounge a chair." And she sat in it, utterly silent, con-
ducting herself with uncanny flair that expressed itself in tiny
variants of what seemed consummate understanding. Silent
she was one of us, later than Last Lisa, cogently alert.

A Black Maria

One day in August sitting by the window of my attic apartment on
Cahuenga Boulevard . . .   —*Michael Bergstein, "The Black Maria"*

✎ Thou Swell

Two notions have begun to war in my mind,
the first a prosaic thing about having to attempt two manuscripts per session lest anyone get left out (entirely reasonable
squawk to follow; it has always been thus, with increased work
after midsemester, especially when you seem to have, now and
then, more than the prescribed dozen in class). The other notion, a pretentious and reckless thing, has taken me back to
Eliot's essay on Seneca, where he quotes (and translates) like
this: "*Fatis agimur; cedite fatis*; the fates drive us—give in to them."
Now, how many shades of cosmological bigotry have intervened
between that dreary *pensée* and this, from Aeschylus's *Prometheus*?

HERALD: *Submit, you fool. Submit. In agony learn wisdom.*

Is there any difference at all, or does the presence of bad old *anagke,* on whom I seem to be harping these days as he tells the gods what to do, change everything? I mean, if the gods are submitting, why not ape them? This is one of the apocalyptic backgrounds I want to wheel up to Michael's West Coast story, with its metallurgical sheen and modish allusions—something about the idiocy of human pretension. Or should it be the heroic triviality of it?

Compared with my next notion, a third, this is chintzy backdrop indeed. I have been looking forward, in the strictly spectatorial sense, to the time when the red giant sun will have wiped us out, our arts and letters too, except that sprightly observers elsewhere have perfect record of our mental doings, and now they will be able to review all our languages as dead ones, contemplating our squeaking and huffing and puffing, our blissful indignation, as a single unit, as, if you like, an artifact in toto. Their express brains will scrutinize the unrolling, then stilled record of a protesting amenable species, from a distance classifying and correlating until they have, of the late great planet Earth, a vision comparable to some such study as R. W. Chambers's *The Continuity of English Prose:* all in one volume, an obstreperous outgrowth. Won't they be amazed by the sheer bulk of our ravings and what amounts to the philately of human conditions? What was all this writing and composing and painting *about?* What was the need for it? What kind of spillage was it? Sap? Vomit? Ectoplasm?

I try a version of these ideas on the group and sense a cold lattice beginning to grow upward from the table as they perceive I have taken their lives-to-be and twisted them into a futile knot. I have preempted their future. "What then of Michael, whose view of hand-me-down chic makes a keen point having to do with comfort? His hero is both a bum and a dandy, aggrandized by his boat on wheels yet spooked by his routine work as barkeep and florist's hack. We turn to the story with clinical relish, suspecting its pattern is that of the young prince denied his inheritance then suddenly granted it, even if only once. Something more powerful than his longing for the bar girl, and even my own esoteric prattlings about Seneca, Aeschylus, and the view from Alpha Centauri: Mrs. Shepard's dead collies, to be driven back East, the dead to the moribund, *leaving a new life behind me on one side and approaching a much older one there in front.* As Michael says in his Fitzgeraldian finis. This is the man who has just written of aerodynamic freeways, puissant heat, and Gabby Hayes redux—surely a chap with some joy in him, a certain rambunctious smarts. "So, what is he doing, ladies and gentlemen, committing himself to two freeze-dried collies? Doing what the variously spelled Mrs. Shepard (Shepherd) asked him to do just because she asked him? In planting Mrs. Shepherd and keeping her in reserve, has he built an inexorable pattern—the dragon call of the East, the big spider suck of dead Cleveland? Is he as trapped as Seneca's Hercules? Is he moving within a pattern that offers him a brief pop but just as fast snaps him back into line? He doesn't fight the dog urge; he says *I knew then that I would fetch Mrs. Shepard's dead collies.* Is it because he suddenly finds life's bliss tawdry? Just another dull hoop to toss his body through, or has he succumbed like an Evelyn Waugh character (see *The Loved One*) to something thanatoptical? What failure of nerve has taken place? I find this aspect of Michael's 'The Black Maria' engrossing, and less fathomable than, say, Henry James's bitter story 'The Beast in the Jungle,' in which John Marcher waits and waits for, metaphorically speaking, the beast of wonder and ecstasy to spring out upon him from the jungle of life. If you like, a god enthusing him. But no, the beast never springs, maybe because it was never there for him, and he dismally recognizes that the wait—allegorically put, *The Wait*—was his portion and would ever be so. Now *that* we understand, and I don't think Michael's story must yield in any way to a superior taint of misery. It's just that he gives us less to work with. Perhaps he grows up in the story, at appalling speed, and by the time it's over has passed rapidly through all the standard positions on the time line from hope to despair. You fall in love, only to embrace a couple of taxidermist's collies. Not L.A., but Cleveland. Not glamour, but *Cleveland.* Maybe, because he has found his right level in the battered barge of a 1942 Custom Super Eight by LeBaron. To aim for the girl is to aim higher. Or perhaps he's aiming higher than Lauren is. I don't know, but his narrator reminds me of those Victorian sages who struggled to find something in life that was not there, and about which those who found it were deluding themselves. So, Michael, you've made me think. I suppose it all depends on your view of Cleveland."

"He certainly gets across the indecisiveness of so-called modern man, I mean modern *human.* I don't think it's a story of incertitude so much as one about the perpetual shiftings of trivial things. Books abide, but Duesenbergs rust." Mark.

"Aren't they mountains in South Africa, where the wild amaryllis grows?" I won't say who.

Nobody wants to answer anybody, or even respond with the sort of reciprocity you get from oriental elephant balls that make bell-like chimes as you shake them. "Yes, they do rust," I say. "Not in South Africa, though."

"I was wondering," I go on, "how the story would be shorter, if the whole thing became more abrupt, less modulated. I get the feeling that Michael wants us to enjoy it qua story even while he's making his disturbing point. What do you think?"

"I don't see why," says Last Lisa, "he can't have both. What's wrong with entertaining readers while making them walk the plank? Dickens." Well said, I think.

"I don't agree," says First Lisa, "if you've written a searing, disabusing story, then it's no use tricking it out with agreeable little tassels, is it?"

I am thinking about two friends, two outstanding women I know very well, and they meet after quite a long time, not having met over Christmas, and they each buy the other a gift just in case. But who will show her hand first? Each has carefully considered the possible behavior of the other. What, I wonder, will happen if neither is willing to show her hand, and they meet some other time, confessing to the ruse, each having lugged the intended present away for fear of having embarrassed the other? Life is made of such contretemps, no matter how well intended, never mind in what good heart. This is the dubiety that grazes friendships: inability to read the other's mind beyond a certain point, when impulse founds itself on sophisticated guesswork. End of reverie. They are taking Michael to task.

"He doesn't really like the woman."

"He wants a less romantic relationship."

"She's too familiar, she's waited too long. *He's had* to wait too long. He only went through with it because there had been so much preliminary he didn't want wasted."

"What a fuss! He's a born philanderer."

They won't deal with the taxidermied collies, carefully installed along with Mrs. Shepherd as the piece's booby trap. "*Taedium vitae,*" I say. "His narrator's weary of life, at least of that life there in the bar, ferrying flowers."

"We can tell," says Vince, contorting his brow as if to dislodge a bad attack of astigmatism, "he's afflicted by the sameness of things. Everything he touches save the booze and the flowers is secondhand. He wants a fresh life, and if he doesn't go into astronomy or chocolate making, he won't ever get it, if you see what I mean. Henry James is apt enough, but in the opening para we read that he has come to L.A. *to think differently and recreate myself in an exotic geography.* I'm a bit puzzled by the last sentence in para one. Can he not see what had brought him what he calls this unfocused need? Or does the prose mean he couldn't see it, though anybody else could? In other words, if you'll bear with me: Are *that which* and *this unfocused need* one and the same, or is the *need* the object of *brought?* They're not the same thing. Is the *need* in apposition or is it the object? The comma's the thing that's wrong."

I'm nodding; the comma has to go, and it has to read either *I couldn't see what had brought me this unfocused need* or *I couldn't see what had brought me, this unfocused need.* The first go seems at one remove. The *what* precedes the *need,* whereas in the second go the *what's* the *need.* "Michael, which shall it be? You have to help us. Or is it deliberately ambiguous?"

"Not in your presence it's not." Maybe what he's getting at here is a so-called midlife crisis. Of course.

"Midlife crisis," I blurt, "that's what it's about. The need is appositional, as Vince said. I wonder if we can persuade Michael to substitute *what* for *that which.* No, we must leave him alone, to flounder or fume. Remember, folks, he, not Michael but his hero, is astride a fulcrum. His journey is between youth and Rutgers *and* career and accomplishment. He really is a John Marcher, but his wait is more active, he believes every bit as much as Marcher does in some bright and beautiful next act, but he takes the initiative in driving away east. This was just another new life, exhausted, and he may go on to yet another, whereas for John Marcher it's all *kaput*; the beast in *his* jungle has been taxidermied, too. But at least Michael's guy drives away with it, perhaps to use it as the prow figurehead on some North Carolina pig farm."

"It's a worrying story. It was worrying before, but now you've made it more so." Sally recognizes the story's power to seep and invade, to get you out of whatever good mood you were in, so as to puzzle out this poor bastard's future. "I think it needs an L.A. tempo," she adds, "not as if all life in L.A. moved that fast, it doesn't, but we need that slap in the face."

"Like a gallon of poodle piss." Someone extemporizing.

"I like it when he sits at the window and looks out at it," I say, "and then *she* looks. Then he dreams about it. That strikes me as authentically American: the vision of promise abortive or not, the temptation not so much to exist, as Cioran cleverly says in one of his titles, as to dream. They can't stop you from dreaming. Thus opens up the entire arsenal of dreaming, which Michael doesn't get into, though he well might. Imagine: you have the thing, it came before you dreamed about it. When you dream about it, you want it to be more of itself, you yearn for accoutrements, say. The dream is not the manifold of desire; it's the foil. The American dream dwindles down to what you get instead of an American dream. Maybe the story is acutely about that—not so much what he wants in the flesh as what he wants to dream about. He cannot dream the dream he wants. My god, it's a Borgesian conundrum after all. His dream is dreaming him. Some inferior person is dreaming him. Sorry, I got carried away. Michael, I like the big tips. You might do more with them. You know what Reagan said about America? It's where everybody can make a lot of money. Is that blue dahlia a reference to Alan Ladd, whom they stood on a box? *Rollicking sea,* fine. Maybe too good-humored. Beckett likens it to hammered lead. I like your dirty hankie, maybe because I did one of those myself in the orbit of Jack the Ripper, chronically encrusted with pale green syrup from a score of indistinguishable colds. I wonder how deep you dare go into him without overloading." Michael shakes his head.

The Planck

And then it comes over me again, the ravaging sense that all I am doing is grooming these brave souls for the plank: walking it. The better they write, the worse their fate will be in a world in which all bad writers write alike the same corrugated cardboard prose without even thinking about it. Who are Sir Thomas Browne, Rabelais, Beckett, Nelida Piñon, Clarice Lispector, Woolf, and Sarraute, to them? I am a species of Nero, good at his trade, but fiddling while Literature burns and the amount of it undertaken by successive generations becomes smaller and smaller. Some fabulous idol of sentence perfection (to name only one facet) lures us on, especially in this, as I've said, an unliterary society that heeds not its belletrists, certainly not as Robbe-Grillet, Pinget, Claude Simon, Duras, and Sarraute were once regarded in France, where they still care about what *we* care about, though less than before. In a sense, there is no need to push farther; they have all achieved a commendable standard, all good enough to oust the best-sellers, which they are unlikely to do, not if they stick to their aesthetic ways. If there's a battle of the books, it was over long ago with the arrival onstage of a huge skim-reading public that cares no more about sentences than about how an ostrich wipes its rear. These are the condom readers, I suppose, to be seen at airports and on planes, racing ahead through their page-turners to a destiny as illusory as the one at the end of their 500-miles-an-hour charge.

We, of course, are concerned with art, less with the spare and lean and taut and brisk and speedy and monofilamental (the prose of haste) than with art which takes its time and even envisions a patient reader who sometimes doubles back, as you must, say, at the end of Beckett's *The Unnameable,* to take in and again prepare for the anguished, strangled death rattle of that interminable-seeming last sentence. Yes, *art,* which brings with it a hint of the perfect. I once told an astronomer friend that I hoped to write some perfect sentences, and he answered that it didn't seem like much, he had no doubt written thousands of them himself without feeling awed. Well, we will be peddling rubies to glassware merchants, whose primary color is green, and therefore a minority who have to stick together, setting up a few superb standards and putting into our prose whatever harmony the composers have left over to us. People with seventy, or even two hundred, channels to suck their advertising from are not going to attend to the French New Novel, the Latin American Boom, or the cloudy accomplishments of postmoderns. I see one or two of my crew here slipping through to Mammon, but not the rest, who if they survive will play the still, sad music of humanity until they drop, courtesy of such as me, high-register belletrist, who warns them of a backlash against fiction for not being "true." Was this going to be the last time they would have for being stylish, of accumulating sentences not nondescript? Was I jumping the life to come? Who knew the future that well? Only someone who had watched the spirit and nerve of the publishing *profession* dwindle and rot over the last two decades. What on earth were they going to? I decided I had best not linger on what I knew, however exact it was. We should be living for the day, seizing the sentence in its full, thick power as the introit to the next one, just as strong.

"I forgot, Michael, that sometimes a story works better back to front. I mean if you stick the last para up front and thus create the whole thing as a retrospective tail. Or, and this is more extreme, just reverse the order of all the sentences in the story, giving it a special feel, like a motor running down, and the so-called climax, if one at all, sending out little streamers. The movie runs backward. If I may." I begin to read the end of "The Black Maria" aloud, in reverse order, beginning with the final sentence:

> "But once in possession of the briefness by which passion is defined I knew what Lauren meant, that nothing was ever enough, and I knew then that I would fetch Mrs. Shepard's dead collies and drive back East after all, stopping only a moment at the divide, leaving a new life behind me on one side and approaching a much older one there in front. I had reached the most that California would ever be. . . .

"And so on. I imagine the person to whom, suddenly, this seems effective is the one who has already read the story in the correct way. As soon as you hit *I had reached,* something appears to give way, wobble, and denature itself, until at last you reach the original first sentence—*One day in August sitting by the window of my attic apartment on Cahuenga Boulevard . . .* The story this way ends with *teasing my senses like thin soup.* It's as if it had become one huge blah-blah paragraph, in other words, a routine and expected explanatory paragraph following one uttered by some kind of color commentator intent on stark phenomena and vivid images. I don't think the story better for being this way, though better than it would be if (following the examples in Beckett's *Watt*) we took the words in each sentence in backward order, which would yield *front in there one older much a approaching and side one on me behind life new a leaving. . . .* Sometimes this trick, fortified by some expedient omissions, yields up a few lively phrases (*one on me behind life,* say). If we follow the insane Watt, an endearing brilliant bumpkin of a character, we run into genuine monkey chatter that can sometimes be unusually moving—*tnorf ni ereht eno redlo hcum gnihcaorppa.* It's almost like *Beowulf* or someone deter-

West's sketch of Beckett's Watt

mined yet uncouth, hell-bent on making an oral sound. These moves do not so much corrupt language as air it out, giving us fresh perspectives. Watt is poignant because, in Beckett's own terms, he has reached a point at which he has to express without having the means to express, though I would say he has plenty to say when all he can manage is a funambulistic stagger of the mouth. Michael is not Beckett, of course, and what 'The Black Maria' gains from such party games is perhaps no more than an architectonic glitch. Never mind, it is good to see English undressed now and then, even in so mild a shift as this, when we move from

> "The Blue Monkey was a fun place to work. The patrons tipped well, and the food was filling. We had a lot of regulars and there wasn't ever any trouble.

"to

> "We had a lot of regulars and there wasn't ever any trouble. The patrons tipped well, and the food was filling. The Blue Monkey was a fun place to work.

"From a priori to a posteriori. There is often, in fiction that calmly assumes its own dignity, an abolition of time, perhaps the same as happens in metaphysical poetry, Donne's rather than Cowley's. The way up becomes the way down, although nothing as astounding as the French translation of *Else a great prince in prison lies,* which becomes the syllabic quacking of *Sinon un prince est prisonnier,* minus all reverberation and clang. That, however, is an extreme version of what I call the mirror problem, after Frank O'Connor's notion of realism as 'the mirror in the roadway.' Sometimes, as in Joyce, several versions of the same event, the same report, mingle and surfeit us: *Next she greesed the groove of her keel ... with ... turfentide and serpenthyme ... ,*" which delights the opportunist, goads the boob. Speaking of boobs, you might let that reversed-letter utterance beginning *tnorf ni ereht*"—I am improvising the pronunciation of my grotesquerie—"haunt you over the weekend. Say it's the first spavined outburst of some poor devil in the Gestapo cellars who has just had his tongue cut out. Or the cellars of the Inquisition. Then *redlo hcum* might mean *regular scum* (if we allow English) and *gnihcaorppa* be the poor devil's grunt for the abomination just inflicted on him. On such horrors does Beckett build his ineffable paradise of the mental home. What?"

They are staring at me as if I have not actually read *Watt* some dozen times and often wonder why no renegade director has never made a movie of it, with all its hallucinations and boorish pantomime, and the lovely trumpet voluntary of Ar-sène the sentimental mailman. "Anyway," I tell them, "wake up your English now and then. Give it a run for its money before they chop the naughty bits off you. You might also consider the role of repetition in narrative prose. I mean Michael might make his character here more of a repetitious oaf. I mean, say you have a person who, whenever he sees a speck of paper on the rug or sidewalk, feels obliged to kneel and, after wetting his middle finger, lifts it up to dispose of it. How many times would you need to demonstrate this? Be careful."

Completeness of Hinterlands

Remember, Joshua, when the grass frogs hit the water and fizzed, making a hissing sound like a soda bottle opening, and then boiled to death in just a couple of seconds, their brown silvery skin emitting tiny bubbles of gas, frog fingers skinny with rounded tips, spread out as if preparing for a priestly blessing. —*Nomi Eve, "King of the Miasma"*

Sistines

After hunting what feels like big game, I turn to Nomi Eve's solid, Latin-lover's piece with an experienced marksman's eye. White hunter back from the *Veldt-schmerz*. "Completeness of hinterland," I say, "is something few writers aspire to, or even try to aspire to. It's when they hope to get the damned thing over as soon as possible, with minimal probing, eavesdropping, speculation, and passion for irrelevance. To her infinite credit, Nomi doesn't lose her patience, but builds and builds. She dotingly lingers on her character, as if, at another time, she might go back to wring from him yet another shade of feeling, the chance of another shot in the dark paying off in the form of a hitherto unnoticed foray. I suppose this Proustian,

Faulknerian tendency, rare enough, has to do with seeing any human life as an inexhaustible object of contemplation, surely the right vision for the novel, even the long short story if you can swing it, but in the wrong hands, present company excepted, a source of tedium because few novelists, writers, have the power of selective epitome. Nomi, without going to excess, provides enough, and thus sets herself apart from those merely diagrammatic, contingency-obsessed writers who scant everything: trim theorem instead of loose baggy monster. I am talking about the proffer of plenitude, which tells you she is doomed to be a novelist. She doesn't know when to quit. The material she gets down jerks more material into view, actually creating it, if you believe as I do that imagination feeds on imagination. So, good. You might sometimes wish she would leave him alone and consider someone, something, else, but she doesn't, and this particular mode of incessant vocative works, through a special kind of overload, like someone summoning up the dead. What do we have here? A voice calling up a presence in countless ironic but affectionate ways, ever conscious that the medicated child, or in this case the unmedicated child, has a special genius for drawing. It's the camp counselor's distinct nightmare, I suppose: one of the charges clearly marked out for excellence, but otherwise a pain in the neck. You can see the prototypical artist getting his onions ready while the writer-artist looks on and worries. OK?"

Not a word, not even from Nomi, who is looking down at the unscored table. I must remember, I tell myself, she is the one undergraduate here, an actual veteran of Tiananmen Square, beyond her years, not for her *favonians* and *lucubrations* but rather incidental close-ups that carry a whole climate with them: "a candy-teased, softly farting child in a supermarket." Not quite a phrasemaker, though on the edge of that privileged status, she is a phrase accumulator, and in my book the surfeit has almost the same effect. Here is someone ostensibly enacting the camp counselor calling up a ghost (who almost certainly is due to have other fictional appearances) while fretting—*wittling* as my mother used to say—so much so that the worry turns the effort into a repeated assault in which, by simple seepage and osmosis, the character fleshes himself out. A nifty technique. I say so, and they still look me in the eye amiably, but turned to stone. Perhaps I am speaking Sanskrit. I ask. They say no in Sanskrit. I go on, knowing the dam will break sooner or later.

"You like Vivaldi more than I do," I tell her. "To me, all his seasons sound like winter, but it's rare to find any allusion to serious music in anything written by anybody under forty. You love your Latin, and that's all I am going to say about it. You must be the only Latin scholar in the group. Against it, one day, you will pit the entire resources of Anglo-Saxon vocab and thus double your output. You will write *fussy lucubrations* and that will be that. Time and again you do useful things amounting to mise-en-scène with commonplace things, the chewed-on pens, for example, taking care to distinguish *chard* from *mica.* What will you do next? *Writhe with a precocious palsy* is what you do next, and I like it fine. Mastery of the short sentence doesn't come easily, but, once you've called it out of the flock, it comes and enables you to rest on a microcosm. What I do like is the way you juxtapose modes. You give us *writhe with a precocious palsy* right next to another quite different utterance that recalls how you cussed out Paul Feeker and threatened to dump his cubbies. If you keep doing this, as it were plaiting the strands, you will have constant contrast, and that's the name of the game. Why, you may even be forgiven your Latin because you in effect smother it in mundane stuff like pale peachy skin. This is really a dossier brought to life, with enough self-aimed rhetoric to establish you as a more than conventional narratorial presence. I'm pleased. I like the variety of your calls to Joshua, certainly the resourceful imprecations (ha!) of someone who knows him well and will try almost any vocal device to get him off his fictional butt. Your daring comes on strong too, most of all when you turn it on its back and write a willing, Latinate attempt to name the unzipped fly in *the custom-tailored, fine woven, double-breasted, suit of you.* It's amusing that the supposed-to-be consumed Ritalin figures here as an abstract presence off, but isn't being taken at all—only a ghost of Banquo's ghost, so to speak. Good. There's something else. Yes, Michael?"

"Were you going to cite her previous convictions?"

"No, only her serious ones."

"Then how about what I'd call her lions in a lion's pelt?" I peer at him as if he has just returned from a naked climb up Everest, scan the pages a moment and pick on a sentence: But I see now (page 10) *"for every festering artifact we unearthed and cremated as if on a Ganges pyre, whole cankerous cages full of petrified silverware and mummified pets remained entombed inside of you."* Near the bottom of the page. "So, Michael, how about that, say? Will that serve?"

"It surely will," he says with skeptical good humor. "How does an artifact fester? Wouldn't it have to be organic? Could you cremate the inorganic? How can a cage be cankerous? Isn't silverware petrified to begin with? Isn't this flamboyant use of language really a misuse? Shouldn't it have, oh, no epithets at all? I mean: *every artifact, cages full, silverware* all on its own. Do I detect here an urge to use words for their own sake, just because they sound so good? It would sound good even without the epithets. Here endeth the first lesson."

"If I had to make a case," I say, "I'd argue that she got so bored waiting to use *festering, cankerous,* and *petrified,* she used them anyway to lighten the load."

Nomi's puckish countenance cheers up. She has spotted a fellow malefactor.

"Can I move on, may I? In certain places she constructs what seems a small bestiary (*daring dolphin fish to mate with shy antelope*), which suggests the presence in her head of set pieces that will fit in almost anywhere if shoved. I have nothing against set pieces. There's one on page 15, actually, not necessarily the best of them, but adequate for purposes of discussion. Listen:

"The squeaking laughter of a skeleton wearing a blue-and-red beanie; a tale told of the upper-left incisor of an Italian mathematician; the decomposing sigh of the circumcised tip from the penis of a future psychopath serial killer; the liquid snicker of your eyeballs constricting as they tandemly settle into your habitual glare; the thirsty braying of a rabid mule bound for Graceland through a back door.

"It's all right, but it isn't top-flight stuff. Maybe a bit lazy. The principle of it's almost as interesting as the component bits. I think it comes from Calvino. It's mild, Nomi, not yet raised to an almost unendurable level of lexical precision. The eyeballs work well, but seem to belong to an ongoing narrative chunk, not microcosmic enough. Any reference to Graceland is bound to be trite unless you break with cliché and say, oh, *he could never make up his mind about bathroom reading: Proust or Sax Rohmer.* . . . Anything to break the mold. But if you had a woman in a fish-smelling crushed velvet jacket getting silver feathers etched onto her pearlized paper-clip-length nails, it might come to life more, away from honorable service into phenomenal acuteness. See?" She sees, knows that "a hematite glow sifting promiscuously through" is better because more original. "I am not sure that, here and there, you don't, as you say, uncork your vintage bottle of self and, not quite reverting to old bad habits, let loose, letting all that's really you, as you say, flow into the work. We all do it, but it's noteworthy to find you expounding the theory and practice already. You think the stuff you've saved up is what matters, whereas, didn't Doctor Johnson say something along these lines?—it's the other stuff, the mortar not the bricks, that matters. I don't altogether believe this, but it sometimes happens, especially with such a straightforward writer as Graham Greene, who no more has set pieces than he has altars cached in his fly. Sometimes, it's the matter-of-fact telling that counts. I defend to the death your right to think so, but I hoot at it from the bleachers because that's what *anybody* can do, whereas to take one neighboring phrase (don't you love to take a neighboring phrase?), *Sistines never seen,* when you compress an entire world into three words, all depending on context of course, you're really getting the job done. Mesmer comes out well."

"Is he related to Klezmer?" Who was that, needling us?

"Let me just add," I say, "that he who fingers his sharpener may go on to sharpen his finger. Page 18. Bottom. Time I desisted and gave the amphitheater over to you all. Do you like this piece?" A few scattered comments begin, from soldier ants to holy hymens, with nobody quite pitching "King of the Miasma" into focus as a viable work headed for the never-say-die Rialto.

Epitomes

Now the logjam threatens to break, if logjam it was. Were they showing a bit of pique at having an undergraduate among us? I have to balance out in my own mind the eagerness to produce of Nomi versus the reluctance to speak up of those who haven't yet offered work. No, that's not the way it is at all. How often one misconstrues a fluke, seeking sense where there's only a random combination of atoms and genes. Christina starts to worry about what she calls "splurge," intending the zeal to overdo and overstate, although this comes with diminished force from anyone who's not read Rabelais or Joyce, Mervyn Peake or Wyndham Lewis. What is she saying?

"It all has to do with proportion, ratio. Some themes do demand the extra, the excess, especially themes that dwarf the presentation, natch with short story, but sometimes even novels don't offer enough room."

"Are we," Mark chips in, "back to trilogy already? Thomas Mann would have agreed with you."

On she goes, apparently heedless, her flame lit. "In this instance, we seem to have an overload of actual repetition, which is all very well, but I detect the same impression of the kid in different versions of him, not a development of the narrative push toward the subtler, more interior parts of his conduct, if you see. This makes, would make, a novella of a vignette, and I seriously doubt, even granted Nomi's liking for verbal flash cards, not necessarily a bad thing, I doubt as I said, the need to embroider his truth in the interests of more fine phrasing. I wouldn't usually talk like this, but here I have to. I think it's a matter of proportion, with the obvious overstated and the implication skimped. It could be shorter, pithier, much more spiritual. Wouldn't this rate as an almost behavioristic story?"

Me, I am dreaming of a common event in which someone gives someone else the finger, middle digit of course, only to receive a full fan of fingers in return with the unuttered retort, "Treat the whole family." This is a nobler occasion, I hope. First, silence, and now the gloves come off. OK. I never promised them a rose garden. Nomi has gone to dwell in silent interiority and looks likely to stay there. I don't blame her.

Dimitri follows up, suavely reiterating the point, but asking to trim the prose, although his own prose, in a more marmoreal fashion, sometimes goes even further. He too is arguing ratio and decorum, which I am willing to ignore in the interests of finding out more about the narrator. Why so clearly female, I wonder? Would it not be better if a male? Dimitri gets off his point at last, having elicited no support, and at once propounds a more interesting theory about how certain works, without actually putting the reader through an enactment of scenes, refer the reader to a context outside the work, in which the story might cogently belong. My goodness, can this be the old theory of the unincluded part, as in Eliot's *Waste Land*? It makes sense that, rather than spelling it all out, one would flash a few cards of a possible context, as Nomi does on page 22, with her ants, in a touch worthy of Joyce Cary, who would have spelled it all out in his humdrum fashion. It has to do with the confidence of the writer, and, I suppose, the pliability of imagination. She does it again on page 29, rather more forcefully, with her Roman clock, the "Fuck you" egg carton, the five-inch worm, the mask of Captain Kirk, the gutter, the fingernails of a dead grandmother, and then curses in pig Latin, the narrator's own full-lipped face, the severed hoof of a horse, the stroller of an abducted baby boy. Seems to me this is an excellent way to compress a culture, even one homemade; it wouldn't be needed in a novel, but in a long-ish story it provides resonance and *durée* just when it's needed, limning the longer story we might have had. If theory it is, it works well in practice. Is this Dimitri's point? If it's really the excluded middle, so be it. If the kid's mother has just spoken "in horrible hieroglyphics," "words parched of affection, mumbled and monotone," and Joshua himself has a "private Argus," then surely in the ambit of prized allusions we can have a capsule version of several unreal cities. Baudelaire, meet Calvino, who should really have been a novelist, unlike John Cheever.

"I respect the motive," Dimitri is saying, "but I wonder if the presentation isn't a bit bald. Doesn't it require some phasing in, some connective tissue? I suspect she enjoys these epitomes so much that she just aches to slot them in, which is OK, but a bit disjointed in effect." I don't see the force of this. After all, we are busily exploring the mind and life of all the Joshuas, and what's the problem with sliding an epitome into his daydreams? Nomi isn't writing a letter to him, she's staging a choral recitative to all his selves past and present, including those unknown. This is fiction after all, not documentary. The narrator who talks of a potent aphrodisiac in remote corners of New Jersey and thus creates an ironic counterpoint to the "real" story, extemporizing from the glue that holds frogs together, has a right to add out-of-time sequences to her facetiousness. So I think.

Can Dimitri be making this point merely for the sake of effect? Does he actually side with her? If you have witnessed the mother "tilting with pregnancy," you are entitled to explore her too, taking whatever chances you prefer. I break into speech, seizing a lull. "I am just mulling over the effect on the story's proportions of (a) abbreviating it, and (b) larding in more of those vignettes seen through a stained-glass window. I think the net effect would be three-dimensional, like those images they call holograms. Too many frogs in this, I think, and I suspect the bonus of a recently read book. The world of frogs is more remote from the story, isn't it, than that of Alexandria falling? Unless, as king of his miasma, Joshua is a king frog. I think Nomi is dealing with a specialized world of frogs and a bigger world, instantly more recognizable, made up of compressed history, from the trivial to the sublime. I also wonder if, granted your first-person narrator, it might not be enterprising to have the male or female narrator change perceptibly during the telling and come out the other end as changed by Joshua as Joshua has remained the same in spite of all interventions. I see nothing amiss in having narrators changed for better or worse by their subject matter. It's what happens in life anyway, not that I think that ample grounds for a shift in fiction. Let me know, please."

"Agreed." Mark, being terse.

"Later." Sally, unsettled.

"The essence of a world picture," Julia says, determined not to be laconic, "is to show people in the act of changing while, ironically, their picture of the world remains the same. And it is only after they have changed that they come to see how out-of-date their *Weltblick* or whatever the hell it's called has become."

"It sure as hell isn't *Weltblick*," Mark says, reluctant to go further.

"Then let it be that," Julia says, having propounded not so much a theory as a postscript to Oswald Spengler.

"Candidly, Nomi," I add, "I'd do more with the other boys, Toftro and little Poett. Your closing line challenges all who read you, and I suppose predators who prefer living prey refers also to fiction writers, which lets you off all hooks."

Nomi has the face of someone privately reciting a series of Latin declensions and conjugations, her lips roaming the paradigms, though she may well have been mouthing an ancient racial curse on the whole pack of us. It sometimes happens that an unusual story will reduce many members to silence, not that they envy it or resent it; it's simply that they hadn't thought of reading such a story before encountering it, and they work a posteriori, secretly building the story's pattern and nature after the event, and then, weeks later, make an allusion to it as if it were there in the dead center of things familiar. I have seen it often, and it may have to do with someone's designing a toilet brush with a fan whirring at the nonbusiness end. People hadn't thought of it until now, so they take a month off.

"All good points," I say, "which I am sure Nomi will stick in the front pocket of her apron."

"Or," says Mark at his boldest, "she will reenact that scene with Max Reger, when he says to the arts editor of some rag, 'Sir, I am sitting in the smallest room in my house. Your review is before me. It will soon be behind me.'"

"Mark, don't we ration ourselves to only one Max Reger story per semester? I agree that it's hard to keep him out with a quote as good as that. Can't we dig something out of Nietzsche or Jünger to cut our eyeteeth on?" He vows to find out, protesting that I know Jünger better than he does. Perhaps I do.

Chatter

Almost prompted to deliver my Sermon on the Mount about dialogue, I more or less resist, remembering only to plead with them not to suspend the rest of the world while dialogue takes place. "Let the sounds of the world continue," I tell them, "almost like method acting. If you don't, you'll end up with those amputated-seeming, isolated exchanges in which the rest of the world has withdrawn out of deference. Much of the conversation that takes place has a background of assorted noises, and actions too. O for peace and quiet, but not in fiction. I am really talking pseudo-silence as John Cage envisions it for his composition entitled *Four Minutes and Thirty-three Seconds of Silence for Any Instrument.* As Cage saw, during any presentation, of speech or music, there is always extraneous noise, so why not now and then subtract the speaker and listen to the racket that Beckett dubbed 'aerial surf'? The white vacant paper of the page in some of Hemingway's dialogue has virtually no aural equivalent, so perhaps we should be scared of it as we just might have been by what André Maurois, translator and liaison officer to the British in World War I, wrote essays about in *The Silences of Colonel Bramble*—amiable sketches of a taciturn senior officer whose opposite number might be said to have appeared in the sequel, *The Speeches of Doctor O'Grady.* Behold the cold, aloof, lip-bitten British as stand-ins for the deity, and Doctor O'Grady for the voluble Irish across the water. Lord help us, the amiable silences (if) of the putative divinity tend to be inter: -planetary, -stellar, -galactic, and so forth. Perhaps it is enough to remain afraid of an even purer silence suspected by Blaise Pascal but unheard by John Cage."

"Isn't this," Mark asks, "the argument, not from design, but from life? I mean, there might just as well be a convention by means of which all dialogue happens in a vacuum. Not a vacuum, I mean, or there wouldn't be any sound at all, but in a silence. More or less like now." Isn't he now at work on a seventh novel?

"Or as in Greek tragedy," I tell him, "especially during the convention known as stichomythia."

"One-line exchanges," muses Vince. "Also as in Ivy Compton-Burnett."

"As in Ivy," I say, "with enormous wit. Her one-liners happen at breakfast over the marmalade and the morning mail— it used to arrive by seven in the old days. Convenient for novelists and story writers, who could thus import the outside world to eggs and bacon, kippers and toast." The old problem has reared its head again. Do we go ahead into cases, in other words, the next offering, or do we continue with—what is it?—my impromptu, disheveled review of literary practice through the ages? They ask for regimen, but they dote on chapter and verse. So we end up with a medley, shuttling back and forth between samples and precepts. This combination might be all right if images from outside didn't continually arrive, setting my pesky head aflame. I sometimes mention them, as now. "The other day, after silencing boxing on TV, in other words depriving myself of commentary by Teddy Atlas, the fight doctor Ferdy Pacheco, and even Bobby Czyz, I noticed some lettering had appeared on the screen—two words: MUTE and VOLUME, two dopey sisters, I decided, the one silent, the other buxom, pronounced *MOOTAY* and *VOLOOMAY,* like Norns in ancient Scandinavian myth. Surely some enterprising fiction will emerge from this couple." I offer them to the class, and watch them all writing. They do not have TVs, but they spend much of their time at movies. They have not read James Jones's *The Thin Red Line,* but years hence they will see the movie of it, and swiftly dismiss my argument that *Saving Private Ryan* is the inferior work of the two because it's so much a convenient contraption, with outflanking dangling ends folded back into the middle. The postwar veteran Ryan comes full circle when he visits the grave in France of the man who found and saved him.

The Nazi they spare ends up thrusting a knife into the heart of an American soldier with cajoling lullabies. And so on. They twig all this, but, I think, prefer the well-ordered, schematic plot of a *Ryan* to the shapeless incongruities of a *Line*. I like movies too, but I dread the books they come from, or even more the books they get made into.

Anyway, off to dialogue. "There's one dialogue," I announce, "that has almost honorable status and is perpetually being added to, witness my own contribution. It typifies American speech at its most contorted:

"Jeet yet?

"Jew?

"Stime.

"Snot.

"Snow use.

"The last line and two others are mine own, otherwise the exchange is a classic of vernacular needing to be extended by at least another hundred lines, yet closer to some dialogue in Beckett's *Watt* than anyone might believe. If this is how the people talk, I'm all for it, truncations and distortions notwithstanding."

"Think of the strain," says Christina. "It would be hard to keep it going on that level for long. Much as one might prefer it."

"Best kept for special occasions," I tell her. "When you need a para that's gravid, loaded, nonportable, and so forth. I mean one that really counts although needing to be read twice. A bit like Nomi's imported capsules of extraneous experience, they tend to be heavily loaded bits of neutron star. What do they say about neutron stars? A thimbleful will weigh a hundred tons or something outlandish."

"All the same," she says, "it would be nice to be able to sustain dialogue in disguise like that all through a story. If language permits. Or slang."

"You've read *Watt,* surely. Well, do, you'll see how Sam does it with all the lexical resources of Trinity College, Dublin, behind him, as well as the best of Irish brogue!"

She vows to ransack *Watt,* which should occupy her a month or two. I hark back to the Greeks, wondering again about the loneliness of stichomythia, with characters committed by the dramatist to pithy one-liners and thereby confined. Restricted. Like one of those parlor games they play on TV, when poisonalities have to conduct a dialogue entirely in song titles: *I'll be calling you-oo-ooh-wooh | Who walks in when I walk out?* (to take two samples from the early twentieth century). Is it that the playwright wants to isolate the characters, more than would be possible if he let them run on in long speeches? I wonder about this, voice it. "What do you think isolates them the more, one-liners or long speeches?"

On the ball, Dimitri answers, "In both cases they're not embedded in a context of narrative."

"Except by the chorus."

"Except by the chorus."

"Isn't there," I ask, "some pathetic, constricting effect with one-liners?"

"Sure there is. They're hemmed in, obliged to fence with bones. They can't go waffling on. I wonder if anyone has done a study of the narrative benefit of the chorus in Greek tragedy. It might be worth doing. I mean, if you collected up all the examples."

They are nodding, as often at some far-fetched notion they will not be responsible for. "Dialogue," I say, as at least once before, "is for the eye, not the ear, so you can twist things around, shift from first to third, paraphrase and précis as much as you like, always remembering the option to change into third whenever it feels stale. I would add that, contrary to the suppositions of those who model themselves on Hemingway's naked, vacant exchanges, mere addition to a statement will three-dimensionalize a speaker, as, say, with someone who sleeps on his left face, over the years pushing up his left eyebrow into an almost vertical tuft so different from the other one, and giving to his every mannerism a touch of incongruous imbalance, as if he were lofting one eye up and winking with the other, inviting you in. That sort of thing can work wonders with what seems impersonal, insufficiently exemplified talk. Remember, as cognitive therapists like to say, there's more to the surface than meets the eye. Explore it, to the tunes of conversation. We can have archaic and eat it, too."

Dramatis Personae

AGHA SHAHID ALI directs the creative writing program at the University of Massachusetts-Amherst. A former Guggenheim and Ingram-Merrill fellow, he has published the poetry collections *The Half-Inch Himalayas, A Nostalgist's Map of America,* and *The Country without a Post Office.* He recently edited a collection of ghazals in translation. He was educated at the University of Delhi and was recently a visiting poet at New York University, working on a fourth book.

DIMITRI ANASTASOPOULOS (Jim) has taught at the University of Albany and now teaches fiction writing at the University of

Rochester. Mammoth will publish his first novel in 2000. He also contributes to *American Book Review* and other journals.

MICHAEL BERGSTEIN, managing editor of *Conjunctions* magazine, lives in the Catskills with his two hounds, Tusker and Rajah. A prolific writer of short stories (*Hamline Journal* and others), he has most recently completed "Cole Porter Delivers a Eulogy at the Funeral of Cleopatra." He wrote down what people said in class, saving what might have been lost.

NOMI EVE (BUCH), after time in China and Israel, having studied at Penn State and Brown, now lives in Cambridge, Massachusetts. Her first novel has been published by Knopf, and foreign rights have been sold in several other countries.

Born in Orange, New Jersey, VINCENT CZYZ was educated at Rutgers and Columbia Universities, has worked for the *North Jersey Herald and News* in Passaic, and shared the Pirate's Alley Faulkner Prize. He founded Voyant Publishing, which published his first novel *Adrift in a Vanishing City*. He now divides his time between Lyndhurst and Turkey.

EDWARD DESAUTELS "lives in the wilds of Somerville, Massachusetts," seeking a publisher for his first novel. Winner of an AWP award in 1994, he has had fiction in *Hayden's Ferry Review*.

JULIA ELLIOTT, of the madcap learned prose, began her education at Duke, then graduated MFA at Penn State, since when she has become one of the vanished though no doubt not the irrecoverable.

DAVE KRESS received his MA in English from the University of New Hampshire and an MFA in fiction from Penn State. He is presently a PhD candidate in English at Penn State, writing about fiction and science. His stories have appeared in *The Little Magazine, Sport Literate, Penguin Review, Slow Dancer, Northwest Review, NRG,* and *Two-Ton Santa.* His first novel, *Counting Zero* (1998) was published by Mammoth Books, He teaches at Roger Williams University and has completed his second novel.

JOANN ROSE LEONARD writes and directs plays for children and teenagers at the Penn State School of Theater. In 2000 Bantam published her first book, *The Soup Has Many Eyes: From Shtetl to Chicago, A Memoir of One Family's Journey through History.* She was educated at Northwestern University and studied mime with Marcel Marceau in Paris. As an actress five feet tall, she has appeared professionally throughout the United States and France in *Rosencrantz and Guildenstern Are Dead* and *L'Histoire du Soldat,* among other plays. She is at work on a second book.

CHRISTINA MILLETTI has been a fellow at the University of Albany, working on a PhD about experimental women writers. Her short fiction has appeared in Scribner's *1998 Best of Workshop Fiction* and the *Chicago Review.* She is also an editor of *The Little Magazine,* an online publisher of hypertext. She is now teaching as an adjunct at the University of Rochester.

TIM MIZELLE, who went on to teach at the University of Alabama, vanished in the direction of the *Paris Review.*

SALLY PONT, whose father is the Yale football coach, is dean of students at Moravian Academy in Bethlehem, Pennsylvania, as well as English teacher and cross-country running coach. Her experiences in this last role occupy *Finding Their Stride* (Harcourt, 1999). She is now working on her second book, about football.

LISA RONEY (Last Lisa) has published fiction in *Harper's* magazine and her first book, *Sweet Invisible Body* (Holt, 1999). She is working on her next book, a novel, and a PhD in literature.

LISA ROSE (First Lisa) has published her first novel, *Body Sharers* (Rutgers University Press, 1993). Her next two books, second novel and a nonfiction work about animals, are due from Crown. She has contributed to various periodicals, including *Feminist Studies* and *Studies in American Jewish Literature.* She is the winner of the 1991 Washington Prize for Fiction and has recently joined the creative writing faculty at Muhlenberg College.

In 1990 the judges for the Elmer Holmes Bobst Award for Emerging Writers, E. L. Doctorow, Denis Donoghue, and Galway Kinnell, chose JOE SCHALL's *Indentation and Other Stories* from a field approximating a thousand. New York University Press published the book in the same year. Joe Schall is working on a second collection and teaches technical writing at Penn State. His work has appeared in many periodicals, including *Flipside,*

The Macguffin, and *The Ligourian.* He is now the Giles Writer in Residence at Penn State, an endowed appointment.

ADAM SCHONBRUN has published several books of poetry and writes occasionally for Israeli newspapers. In March 2001 he presented a one-man theatrical performance of poems from *Kraken Heaven* at the University of Southern California. He is also at work on a first novel.

MARK SEINFELT's first book is *Final Drafts: Suicides of World-Famous Authors* (Prometheus Books, 1999; foreword by Paul West). He has an MFA from Washington University, St. Louis, and is the author of several novels. He is now working on a commissioned study of banned books.

ML   8/01